LET'S MAKE A
CONTRACT

GETTING YOUR TEEN
THROUGH HIGH SCHOOL
AND BEYOND

ANN SCHIEBERT, PsyD

Andrew Benzie Books
Walnut Creek, California

MW00337812

Published by Andrew Benzie Books
www.andrewbenziebooks.com

Printed in the United States of America

Second Edition: September 2018

10 9 8 7 6 5 4 3 2 1

ISBN 978-1-941713-85-3

Book design by Andrew Benzie

Contents

Introduction

"Why is my family such a mess?" "I can't get my teen to do ANYTHING that I expect him/her to do." "Everything is an argument!" "I'm exhausted from trying to explain to my teen WHY he/she must study." "I am ready to pull my hair out!" "I'm ready to quit being a parent!"

Dear readers: I can't tell you how many times I have been sought out by parents to mediate what seems like never-ending issues between them and their young adults! So many parents of teens are at a loss about how to provide loving structure and supportive guidance—especially when it's not wanted by their young adult. The very nature of the American teenager is one that strives for independence and identity. There is an intense desire to make one's own decisions, select one's own friends, try out the "forbidden." The problem is that the part of the brain that enables one to weigh the pros and cons of a choice is not developed yet, so for most teens it is an impossible task to consider consequences when making a decision. Knowing this scientific truth, we, as the guides for the next generation of adults, have the responsibility of teaching our teenagers how to make choices. We have the duty to help them look past their immediate focus and understand that there ARE consequences for making bad decisions.

Consider the many impulsive decisions teens make that become tragic headline news: "Teen Found Dead From Alcohol Poisoning at College Frat Party" "Teen Pregnancy on the Rise" "Teens Die in Car Games" "Teen Dies While Driving and Texting—Kills Family of Four." Each of us has heard of catastrophes caused by young adults who make one bad choice that ruins their lives. All of us know that for most teens who are caught in the consequences of their bad decisions, they wish they could hit "instant replay" and make a different choice.

The many years I have interacted with teens, young adults, and their parents have allowed me to witness the parenting and relationship failures that come from not being exacting, specific, and concise about parental guidelines. I have seen the disappointing results that come from caregivers rendering spur-of-the-moment or after-the-fact consequences for a violation of some unclear expectation. Many parents ASSUME what their young adults "should know." What often follows a violation of some unclear guideline is condescending explanations, arguing, shouting, disrespectful accusations, badgering, and insults. These types of combative and demeaning interactions provide fuel for opposition to future parental limit-setting. They demolish any hope of collaborating with one's teen about cooperation with future expectations.

Another difficulty that arises in the rearing of one's teenager is that many parents think it is loving to rescue their young adult from the consequences of their bad judgments. What this actually teaches one's teen is that there are NO real consequences for their poor choices, because they will be saved from them by their parents. Many caregivers are held hostage by such ideas as if their teen decides not to attend school, it will be horrific if they won't graduate with their class, or if their young adult serves jail time for a DUI, their driving record will keep them from having a successful life. These thoughts provide an impetus to save and rescue and fix. They keep us teaching our teens that they bear limited—or no—responsibility for their actions.

When parents analyze their fearful beliefs that lead them to fix and save, what they find is that rescuing perpetuates the continued making of bad decisions and reinforces the behavior they don't want to support. For example, there are untold numbers of teens who get a DUI and their parent focuses on "how to get him/her off" by hiring an attorney and paying the fine. It has been my experience that a large percentage of these "rescued teens" go out and do it again! Why? Because their parents took on the teen's responsibility and negated the consequences. In contrast, having to face the natural results of bad decisions often provides the lessons that will be the most profound and therapeutic ones for a young adult. Rescuing from consequences reinforces the idea that "my parents will deal with this." Enduring one's consequences for poor judgment encourages change!

I have sat through highly emotional therapy sessions when young adults feel they have been betrayed by their parents because they had no prior knowledge about what "the rules" were and what "the consequences" were for breaking them. The parents of these teens feel angry because they think their young adult "clearly knew the rules" or "should have known" the expectations. The anger that becomes stored up over such disputes can incite mutually disparaging feelings: the teens feel unheard, unguided, not believed, sabotaged; their parents feel disrespected, undermined, ignored, and lost. They feel maligned and insulted by the contemptuous remarks made by their teens. Indeed, it is a power struggle. And parents, without finesse, YOU will not win a power struggle with your teen. Caregivers, you must set aside some of your feelings, and care enough about your teen's future, to change the structure of how you set boundaries and limits. If you don't provide such guidance, every unwanted behavior that your teen exhibits goes into what I like to call the "OK Corral." Housed in the OK Corral are behaviors that aren't OK but were given a pass for various reasons: We were too tired to do anything about it; we were watching our favorite TV show; we didn't want to have a conflict—and on and on. Unacceptable behaviors become acceptable. It is very difficult to get things out of the OK Corral.

So why not make this easier? Why not let all parties involved know, before the event, what the agreements are, and what the consequences are for breaking them? By having consequences that are known up front, the choice to follow guidelines or to select the consequences for ignoring them becomes that of your young adult. With parental expectations and the ramifications for not following them written down, there can be little confusion about what the agreements are.

The purpose of this book is to provide anyone caring for teens and young adults with ideas about how to structure their behavior and how to assist them in making good choices… even if they don't want to. My goal is to simplify what seems complicated. My intention is to provide ideas that will enable our young adults to have successes. Setting boundaries and limits will significantly change your family life for the better. At first, you will have lots of pushback from your teen. If you are firm in your resolve to respect the contracts you make, eventually, most parents are amazed at how peaceful their family becomes. How do I know? I know from the reports of many families who have tried the "Let's Make a Contract" method of behavior modification.

The ideas here are not necessarily new. What is unique are the written agreements, the delineation of responsibilities of all parties to the contract, and the creation of sensible and relevant consequences that are written down BEFORE any violations to agreements occur. This alleviates arguments because it places the entire responsibility for selecting a consequence on the teen.

Whether you have a straight-A student or one who is flunking out of high school and brings chaos into your house, having a contract will make your life better and easier.

So why not try it out?

How to Use This Book

The intent of writing this book was to provide parents and caregivers of teens and young adults with ideas about how to avoid problematical situations before they happen. I also wanted to furnish templates for contracts so our teens would know their parents' behavioral expectations. Another objective was to open the communication doors between teens and their caregivers. Many of us parents get hooked into our teens ever-creative and inventive games of "You Didn't Tell Me" or "I Didn't Know." And, thinking we must be fair, we respond with the explanations of the "You Should Have Known" justification game wherein we caregivers abdicate responsibility for not having addressed the issue before it occurred.

Being the parent of a teen can be very frustrating and tiring. Let's face it, we are busy earning a living, trying to pay the bills, provide for our family, keep our relationships alive, cook dinner, be a good listener, and monitor our growing children, all at the same time. If you are anything like me, I get tired just thinking about it! Teens can't raise themselves. We parents must provide guidance and set limits. Use this book to stimulate ideas for how you can better engage with your teen while guiding them to do those behaviors of which you approve.

Every template in this book can give an opportunity to strengthen your connection with your young adult. Each topic addressed can provide you with ideas of areas that maybe you haven't discussed with your teen. Tailor-make your contracts to suit your family and your adolescent. Interweave humor and fun. Create consequences that are meaningful to your teen. Make sure the consequences are commensurate with the offense: grounding your teen for life is not an appropriate consequence for coming home an hour after curfew. Consider the importance of having your teen know that the consequences for poor judgment will be closely related to the topic of the infractions. For example, if there is a violation of cell phone use, taking the TV away for an evening has nothing to do with the cell phone misbehavior.

In an attempt to be all-inclusive to those of us raising teens and young adults, I have interchangeably used parent(s), caregiver(s), and guardian(s). The scripts provided have been tried in many families, and those caregivers who have used them report great success. The only reported failures that have occurred are when the contracts aren't enforced. If two or more of you are raising a young adult, be sure you are in agreement with the contents of the contract you create. Have you ever heard of the game "Divide and Conquer"? If a young adult has one parent who is complying with the letter of the contract and the other is waffling and not enforcing consequences, guess who the teen will turn to when they seek to avoid enforcement of the contract? This often leads to that proverbial "touchdown" for the teen when his/her parents are the ones arguing about the contract. The teen learns he/she can divert the focus of attention from being on their poor choices to being on their parents having issues with each other about contract enforcement. This dynamic opens the door to manipulation by the teen and increases family stress because of arguments about contract enforcement. It also teaches your young adult that the contract really holds no weight because the words of the parents ("these are the consequences for ____") don't match their behavior (arguing with each other and ignoring that THEY also hold responsibility for contract compliance).

"Teen," "young adult," and "adolescent" have been used interchangeably. However, "young adult" can also refer to someone over 18 years of age.

> **NOTE:** All contracts in this book are available in electronic form to download, modify, and print. See page 210 for more information.

CHAPTER 1

Welcome to High School

Let's remember high school… that overwhelming transition from middle school. Think back to your first day. What comes to mind? For me, I picture being dropped in the center of a foreign country— stuck there with no way out. I don't know the culture. I'm scared. The language sounds familiar but many words hold a different meaning than how I understood them in the past. I still have my guardians and family, but they are not here with me. All of a sudden I am faced with hordes of people I don't know, and I feel very unsure of myself and very, very small. There's no tour guide to lead me through my day; I only have a schedule of classes. Next to each class is a room number and a time for me to show up to get instruction.

I see some of the kids who attended my previous school. Some are laughing but others look scared too. I feel lost. I say, "Hi" in hopes that they'll talk to me, but they are too busy discovering what they are expected to do next.

Day two is better. After a few months, I "get" the culture. I have learned that "Let's party" isn't an invitation to go swimming. It means let's go out and get drunk or high. I've discovered that "have a smoke" has nothing to do with cigarettes and "hook up" doesn't imply that someone has a winch and wants to go for a ride in the snow. From watching and listening to upper-grade students, I learned that "You got a problem?" isn't an expression of care and concern and "You a ho' " is not about finding a gardening implement. Honestly, by the end of freshman year, we 9th graders learn an entirely new and ever-changing language that our parents don't understand.

If I had known all the adjustments ahead of me, I might have opted to stay in 6th grade. But then I would have missed an immense opportunity to grow, mature, learn from disappointments and failures, and feel the elation that comes with successes. I would have been stuck in my 6th-grade manner of problem solving and dealing with emotions. In retrospect, I don't think any of us would opt to remain in our 12- or 13-year-old ways of coping with life's challenges. Here's the question: Knowing of our own ups and downs in high school, and being aware that today's teens face many more challenges than we did, how do we navigate them through these years in a manner that structures their successes, respects their individuality, protects them from their poor judgment, allows for failures, and assists them in learning from their mistakes? I thought you'd never ask!

How our teens survive high school will leave an imprint on them that will affect them the rest of their lives. We guardians of teens weren't given written instructions about how to get our teen through high school with as few ramifications from poor judgment as possible. We parents and families need ideas that can provide a foundation for establishing values, morals, creativity, fun, and a healthy life balance.

There are myriad crossroads that face high school teens. We must strive to be one step ahead of them so we can divert them to the various paths that will help them become self-sufficient adults. You can use the ideas in this book to foster loving, structured growth.

Curfew

For those offspring who are living at home, it can be reasonable to set a curfew. After all, we want our teens to be rested for sports, school, homework, and their jobs. Curfews also teach responsibility. One must be home at a set time: It's the agreement and must be kept.

Let's imagine that my 17-year-old has a midnight curfew on weekends. Friday night, he is late by 10 minutes. What do I do? Ahhh! If I let the 10 minutes slide, am I teaching my son that midnight really means 12:10? YES! When contracts are made, there is no negotiating for change after the fact. That only teaches that the curfew agreements are actually nonbinding.

Differences for weekdays and weekends are usually incorporated into a curfew contract. This allows for greater weekend privileges because a weekday curfew has been respected and followed.

NOTE: All contracts in this book are available in electronic form to download, modify, and print. See page 210 for more information.

Curfew Contract

Agreement	My Responsibilities	Consequences for Breaking Agreements
Weekdays	Teen: Be home by 6:00 P.M.	Teen: Grounded one day on weekend. Parents: If you give one minute on the time home requirement, you open the door for your teen to disrespect your curfew also.
Weekends	Teen: Must be home by midnight.	Teen: Grounded one day on weekend.
Changing curfew	Teen: Inquire about a curfew extension before an event that requires being home later. Get extension in writing so there are no misunderstandings.	Teen: Having to be home at the regular curfew time.
Negotiating	Teen: Be clear about what you are requesting. Better to have it in writing.	Teen: No changes in curfew.
Chronic disregard for curfews (more than five times)	Teen: Comply with this contract.	Teen: Grounded for seven days.

School Attendance

This type of contract is necessary when one has a young adult who is being truant. It there are no consequences for cutting school, then covert permission is granted for this behavior. If a parent or caretaker just throws their hands in the air and says, "I don't know what to do," that teaches the student who is needing structure and guidance that they have stumped their care provider and can keep "hanging out" instead of going to school.

It is important to know that young adults, just like younger children, thrive from having structure in their lives. Structure helps organize time, assists in knowing what to expect next, and provides boundaries for what is—and what is not—acceptable. It is the law that children go to school. Parents are responsible for their child's attendance. The only reason one would need a contract about school attendance is if a student has decided to NOT live up to his/her educational responsibilities.

School Attendance Contract

Agreement	My Responsibilities	Consequences for Breaking Agreements
An education is a family value.	Teen: Study and learn.	Teen: No ability to get a job that will allow you to support yourself.
Student to attend school between 8:00 A.M. to 3:10 P.M.	Teen: Stay on the school grounds and attend all classes. Stay at school the entire time. Caregivers: Will contact student's teachers on a daily basis (if needed) for an attendance report.	Caregivers: If you decide not to enforce school attendance, your teen will be ill prepared for a career, and you will open yourself up to legal consequences for not complying with laws regarding mandatory education. Teen: You will have to face the legal consequences for not attending school. You will not be able to find a good job because you don't have a GED or high school diploma.
Attend school five days/week.	Teen: Arrive at school on time. Caregivers: If attendance agreement is violated, parents will contact the truancy officer and student will have whatever consequences are mandated by that person.	Teen: For any school day missed, one day of weekend privileges will be forfeited. Any tardies will result in home chores of parents' choice for the total amount of time teen was late to school/class.
It is the student's responsibility to wake up.	Teen: Get myself up in time to arrive at school on time. Caregivers: Agree not to nag or rouse teen to wake up. A list of chores will be posted on the refrigerator along with a time expected for completion.	Teen: Anytime student is late to school due to not getting up, student will spend the amount of time she was late, doing five chores around the house such as folding the wash, putting it away, doing the dishes, etc.
Teen: Agrees to willingly complete chores that are the result of student's poor decisions regarding school attendance.	Teen: Complete chores that have been assigned to me due to non-compliance with school attendance agreement.	Teen: Being grounded without cell phone, Internet, or television for the two-day weekend beginning 9:00 A.M. Saturday and ending 9 A.M. Monday.

A School Attendance Contract needs to put the burden of performance on the student. Notice in the contract example above that every consequence is designed to be the result of the student choosing not to follow the agreements. The choice of having a consequence is entirely on the student because he/she knows in advance what the consequence will be. For example, if the student chooses to not set the alarm and to sleep the day away, then the student has chosen the consequences enumerated by that particular agreement. In the contract above, if the student decides not to attend school on one day, then he/she has selected to lose one day of weekend privileges.

If truancy becomes an issue, there are other contracts that can be designed. If a teen decides that they don't care about losing weekend privileges and that they'd rather stay home on a school day and watch TV, the caregivers need to decide how to make that extremely uncomfortable. Many parents lock their noncompliant teens out of the house during school hours. Some hire a "baby" sitter to watch and report to the caregivers exactly what happens during the day.

It is also important to be sensitive to possible reasons a teen/young adult would not want to attend school BEFORE one puts a School Attendance Contract in place. Investigate exactly why your student does not want to be in school. Often there are circumstances at the school that a student doesn't know how to solve, so the solution to the teen can look like not attending school. Below are listed some suggestions for parents to explore:

1. Is your student being bullied? Discuss this with your teen. Bullying presents a problem that is difficult to solve. Sometimes, students feel they can't be candid about what is happening at school because they don't want to "rat" on anyone. Sometimes, fear of retribution paralyzes teens so they don't defend themselves or report bullying.
2. Are there certain staff members at the school who are problematical to your student? Teachers, principals, or other staff can be insensitive. Have there been instances when your teen has been embarrassed by teachers in front of the class? How are your teen's relationships with the school employees?
3. Is your teen experiencing emotional issues? It is imperative to explore the possible answers to this question. Some mental illnesses manifest in young adulthood. Sometimes, the breakup of a romantic relationship can lead to depression. Find out what is leading your teen to not want to attend school.
4. Is your student involved with drugs and alcohol? So many parents close their eyes to this possibility. Drug tests can be easily purchased at the local pharmacy. Instead of wondering, get a definite answer by having your student take one.

Grades

While good grades are desirable, it is really important that pressure is not put on teens to get perfect grades. Parental expectations can lead to anxiety, depression, and feelings that the teen can never be good enough to please the caretakers. Additionally, many parents overestimate the intellectual abilities of their students. If your child has an average IQ, he/she probably won't be in accelerated classes or skip a grade due to academic prowess. Accept that, and create agreements that are attainable by your teen. Setting the bar too high can lead to failure.

There can be many incentives put in place to encourage our students to strive for good grades. Scholastic achievement can be rewarding in itself, but additional motivators can propel students to surpass what even they thought they could do.

The sample contact below is designed for the family that simply wants to provide its student some clarity around expectations. It can also serve to offer incentives for meeting academic guidelines. The Grades Contract serves as a binding agreement between the student and parent. It includes responsibilities for the parents such as providing a quiet study space away from the other activities that might be going on with the rest of the family. It puts parents on notice that there are natural consequences for them too if they break the agreements.

When parents break agreements, it gives tacit permission for the teen to also break agreements. If the parent fails to live up to any of their part of the contract, they are teaching the teen that it is OK to disrespect an agreement. Parents benefit from being mindful about what they actually teach their teens/young adults. The phrase "Do what I say, not what I do" invites disrespect for caregivers. When a young person sees a guardian complying with a contract, he/she will have a role model to follow.

Many of us parents feel overwhelmed by our own lives and jobs. It can be draining to have to follow a structure that has little flexibility. Research shows that most children and young adults do much better with guidelines. They know what is expected of them and of others. There is no guesswork. We parents are the ones who will pave the way for our children. How we follow our part of a contract will determine how our children follow them.

WHEN PARENTS ARE A PARTY TO A CONTRACT WITH A TEEN/ADOLESCENT, THEY MUST BE MINDFUL THAT COMPLIANCE TO THE CONTRACT COMPLETELY RESTS WITH THEM, NOT WITH THE TEEN!

Grades Contract

Agreement	My Responsibilities	Consequences for Breaking Agreements
A GPA (grade point average) of at least a B- is expected.	Student: Complete homework on time, study for tests, ask for help when a subject is too challenging. Parents: Provide quiet time for study, provide and pay for tutors when student requests.	Extra study time during the week and on weekends will be provided for the student.
	Punctuality Complete and turn in assignments when due.	Parents: Will arrange with teachers a system to monitor student's delivery of homework.
	Quiet Time Parents: Will provide a quiet time and place for study. Each school day Monday–Friday from 7–10 P.M. student is expected to complete homework and study for tests/papers. During that time, cell phones, video games, and TV will be off.	Loss of TV or video games from 10:00–11:00 P.M.
	Tutoring Upon request, parents will arrange for student to have a tutor to assist with courses that student is finding very difficult.	Student: Calling a family meeting to address this issue. Natural consequences: student losing faith in parents' word, opting out of this agreement, losing respect for parents.
	Feedback Parents: Be open to help student with ideas for special projects and papers. Listen to their ideas. Collaborate with them. Make it fun.	Natural consequences: Student will become more attached to peers, withdraw from parents, be less interested about papers/projects.

It is further agreed that when a B- GPA is reached, student will have earned _____.
(Make this something they like: a video game, movie passes, out to lunch/dinner, special shoes, etc. This allows the student to feel he/she has earned something special.)

Signed: _____

Signed: _____

High School Attire

What is proper attire for high school students? How do you want your teen to present him/herself at school?

Relaxed?

One outfit fits all?

On the edge?

Suggestive?

Teenie Tiny

There is an old adage: Just because you are invited to an argument doesn't mean you have to accept the invitation. What is really important for your high school student to get safely and successfully through high school? Consider which battles you need to win. So many caregivers of teens enter into the clothing and hairstyle war—and they most often lose this battle. Remember when pink and blue hair were so bizarre that those who dyed their hair those colors would be stared at and considered weird? When did it become trendy to shave one half of your head and have longer hair on the other side? In the mainstream at a high school near you are all sorts of hairstyles in various colors. There are also many types of apparel from miniskirts to muscle shirts to black attire accessorized by huge crucifixes. There are distinct styles that indicate a membership in a subculture. There are colors of apparel that designate a gang affiliation.

Is apparel an area of your teen's life in which you feel you can allocate freedom for expressing individuality? We parents will have to decide when to let go and provide our adolescents with a way to have a voice, a way to make a statement that we might not agree with. Unless you have observed that your teen's choice of attire or hairstyle would put him/her in possible danger, hair and attire are often harmless ways for teens to create an individuality assertion.

Sometimes hair and attire reflect dedication to a subculture. Consider if you think membership in the subculture your teen wants to join is a healthy option. Consider if your teen just wants to dabble in the subculture or if they want to be a dedicated member. There is a world of difference between the two. In order to make informed decisions about that, let's familiarize ourselves with some of the major customs of the more popular groups that might attract your teen:

Emo

The emo subculture represents a way of life that encompasses fashion, an emotional way of being (often associated with despair, sadness, hope, and self-loathing), and a way of behaving. It has been described as a "sad" group. It started in the 1980s, evolved by adding emotional lyrics to punk music, and became a style of living and a way of acting. Usually, teens between 12 and 18 years old embrace the emo subculture.

Emos often have dyed blue/black or dark red hair that is styled in a unisex manner. Hair is cut short and the signature of an emo hairstyle is a long bang that is often longer than the rest of the hair and hangs over one eye. An inordinate amount of gel and hair products are used to keep an emo's hair-do in place. They often wear heavy black makeup that is highlighted with red. Emo attire usually consists of tight black jeans and t-shirts, skate sneakers, tricolored stockings, and an array of bright-colored accessories. A very significant emo accessory is a ring which is placed in one's lower lip, via piercing.

Emotionally, many emos feel that because they can't understand themselves, no one else could possibly understand them. They use poetry to describe their dark and depressive thoughts/feelings and to express their pain. Emos resist the "norm" in thought, word, behavior, and attire. They have been known to cut themselves to relieve frustration. Some emo followers have entertained the idea of suicide to solve their problems. Some have followed through on their dark feelings.

Guardians of teens need to decide if this alternative lifestyle would be healthy for their teen. There are different philosophies. Some teens find it to be a relief to find a group of kids who don't fit in with the "norm." There are groups who focus on being a "happy emo kid." They find comfort in their emo-friends. Other emo groups that focus exclusively on their dark interests and on the sad, unexplainable inequities of life have created depressed, and often self-destructive teens. If your teen is leaning toward the more agonizing, morose, and pessimistic emo lifestyle, they need more attention from their parents and more activities that focus them elsewhere.

Where to follow the emo community? Try Myspace.

Goth

Like the emo subculture, the goth community also emerged from the 1980 British punk rock scene. It is an ambiguous and very diverse subculture, and the goth way of life differs from continent to continent. To generalize, goths seem to attract teens who are experiencing academic and social difficulties, and those who feel alienated from their peers and want to find a way to express their feelings. They enjoy the shock value their attire and hair receive from the mainstream culture. Most goths are very literate and creative, and when engaged are quite likable and intelligent. Many goths have been victims of bullying, or emotional, physical, or sexual abuse and have a dislike for authority. Some are pacifistic, and some are violent.

The goth subculture consists of many subgroups ranging from the "weekenders" for teens who want to try "being" goth on weekends, to the "vampires" who fixate on drinking blood. For more information about goth subgroups go to www.gothicsubculture.com.

Goth attire is highly visible and is influenced by nineteenth-century Gothic literature and contemporary horror movies. Goths dress in Victorian, Renaissance, and medieval attire styles, which are made of black velvet, lace, and fishnets. The attire is often accessorized with corsets, gloves, and silver jewelry that depicts occult or religious themes. They use makeup to pale their complexion, and dye their hair black. Dark eyeliner and fingernail polish are worn by both male and female.

It is important to note that self-harm and suicide have been shown to be prevalent among some of the goth subgroups. If your teen is interested in this subculture, parents might be concerned about his/her feelings of competence, and connectedness with others. Another area to explore is why one's adolescent feels the need to have social and emotional support from an alternative lifestyle.

Ravers

The rave subculture is known for amphetamine, psychedelics, and ecstasy use, combined with laser light shows and all-night dancing to computer-generated techno music. This is said to be in search of harmonious and communal spiritual healing. It is a quest to reach an altered euphoric consciousness that is stimulated by a mix of repetitive percussion and flashing lights. DJs are considered the "gods," and ravers can become godlike as well via entering the euphoria that is shared by the drug-altered participants.

Within the rave culture are two subgroups that are distinguished by which psychoactive drugs are ingested. The *fryers* usually take ecstasy because of its ability to produce a rapid and aggressive psychedelic trance, and the *melters* usually ingest LSD and mushrooms because they tend to calm the body while the mind "trips out."

Rave attire tends to be flashy and scanty. Glow-in-the-dark outfits and fur boot-covers are popular. Ravers suck on pacifiers to keep them from the ecstasy-induced tendency to grind one's teeth.

Menthol nasal inhalers, surgical masks, and neon glow sticks are used to augment sensory perception. Cool-down rooms are provided to help one decrease one's body temperature, which can rise dangerously due to drug use. Raves are usually advertised as "alcohol free." What is not said is that club drugs are plentiful.

If your teen suggests that he/she wants to attend a rave, parents would do well to review the culture of your adolescent's friends and to help them find other outside interests. Please review how dangerous some of these drugs are in my book *Let's Make a Contract: Getting Your Teen Through Substance Abuse*. Of note, ecstasy can PERMANENTLY deplete the brain's serotonin—that neurotransmitter that greatly affects mood, social behavior, sleep, memory, and sexual desire.

Gangs

Bret

Bret was a 17-year-old junior in high school. He lived in a lower socioeconomic neighborhood with his mother and two younger sisters, ages 13 and 10. Bret's mother worked two jobs to support her children and was seldom home. Bret's father was serving an 8-year sentence for domestic violence, assault, and robbery. Bret had been charged with watching his sisters when he returned from school. As a result, he was unable to participate in any afterschool sports or other activities. He had few friends. He felt angry and isolated. Bret stated, "My sisters are bratty, and they don't do what I tell them to do."

Bret was aware of gangs in his neighborhood. He liked some of the guys in a gang who "provided safety for my street." Occasionally, they had invited Bret to share a joint with them, and eventually he felt that "these dudes were my friends." He was able to tell them his problems and how hard it was to care for his sisters after school. He shared that he hated school. After he had admired some Nikes one of his new pals had on, they took him to a store and bought him a pair. Bret felt so empowered; for the first time in his life, he had on some clothing that was a "power statement." Bret declared, "These shoes say that I'm not nothing; that I'm something!"

Bret's new friends also shared some of their personal history with him. Many came from one-parent families. None had jobs. They all thought school was stupid. They talked to Bret about how they now had a close family (the gang) that provided them with money, respect, and protection. They invited Bret to join, and advised him that he'd have to prove himself before he could become a full member of their "family."

Bret began selling drugs. He made a lot of money, most of which went back to "support the family." Now, for the first time in his life, Bret felt he had some power, some pals who had his back, and respect from others. Bret felt like he belonged! He became one of his "family's" most lucrative drug dealers. He wore their colors and got a tattoo on his thumb signifying that he was a gang member. He had passed the first step of initiation. To pass the second step, Bret had to mug people on the street and steal their wallets for cash and rob them of their driver's licenses. Many members of Bret's gang "family" were experts at identity theft, and those stolen driver's licenses made it much easier. Bret passed the second step.

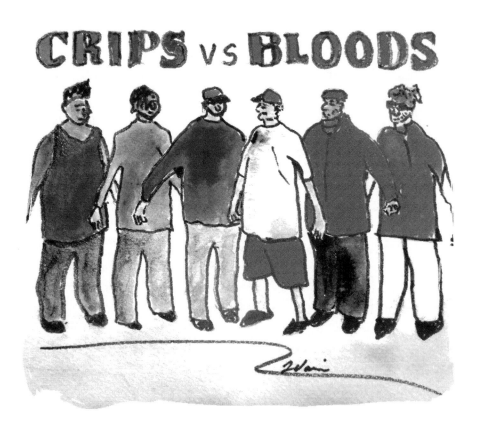

The third and last step one had to pass to become a gang member was to shoot a member of the gang who had control over the adjacent neighborhood. This was an area that Bret's gang longed to control because the retail owners in that neighborhood all paid top dollar for "protection." Bret was not a murderer. He couldn't ask his "family" to give him another option because they would think he was a "chicken" and "disloyal." Such a request would carry with it possible life-threatening consequences for Bret and perhaps even his family. He felt stuck. He began to rethink his "family" affiliation. While he loved his gang brothers, he didn't want to spend the rest of his life fleeing the law. Where does a 17-year-old turn to reverse decisions that are later regretted?

Before we continue on with what happened to Bret, let's review the high-risk factors for gang membership as stated in the August 1998 *Juvenile Justice Bulletin*, "Youth Gangs: An Overview:"

- Lack of jobs for youth
- Poverty compounded by social isolation
- Domestic violence
- Negative peer networks
- Lack of parental supervision
- Early academic failure and lack of school attachment

Bret met all six of the major criteria for being at high risk for gang involvement. The gang appeared to fill in the parts of Bret's life that had made him feel isolated and alone. It provided a sense of family, protection, money, excitement, and he, for the first time in his short life, could appear "cool." Bret's gang gave him a place to fit in and goals to strive for. His gang brothers wore the latest fashions, drove the hottest cars, got seductive girlfriends, and threw the best parties Bret had ever attended. What was not to like?

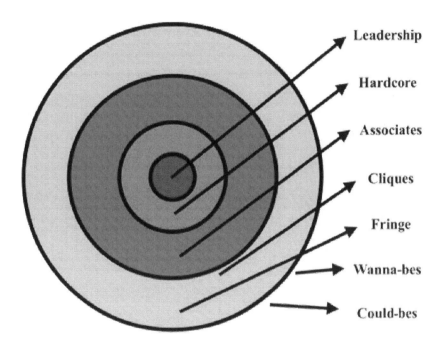

Although Bret's mother, Ida, worked two jobs and was seldom home, she had given her son some values. She made him attend church with her and his sisters every Sunday. Over the years, she and members of the congregation had talked to Bret about concepts such as "good and bad" and "right and wrong." Even though Ida knew that Bret hated going to church, she made him go. When she noticed behavior and attire changes in Bret, she went to her pastor to discuss her fear that Bret had joined a gang.

One Sunday after church, Pastor Franklin approached Bret and asked him to accompany him to his office. There, he expressed concerns about Bret's future. He advised Bret that he suspected him of gang involvement. When Bret inquired why Pastor Franklin thought he had joined a gang, Franklin replied, "Bret! You are wearing expensive clothes. You have a new watch! Your shoes must have cost $150. You have the best cell phone. Who is paying for this? I know your mother well enough to know she could never afford such things!" Pastor Franklin told Bret he was "wise" to him and accused him of adopting a "thug lifestyle" that celebrated criminality.

At first, Bret was defensive. It is dangerous to admit gang affiliation, and by the time of this meeting with Pastor Franklin, Bret had been a gang member for two years. Pastor Franklin was relentless, and told Bret that he knew about an upcoming court date to formally charge Bret with selling a controlled substance. Bret was astounded! He had not told anyone except his gang brothers, who posted bail for him. Did that mean that one of Bret's gang members was a snitch? If Bret came clean, would the "snitch" report back to his gang family? This frightened Bret even more. He didn't know what to do. Bret looked Pastor Franklin squarely in the eye and asked him, "Why should I trust you?"

Pastor Franklin was well versed in gang culture. He had assisted some of his congregation in fleeing their gang. Pastor Franklin had inside connections. He looked back at Bret and said, "You should trust me because you are on the precipice of ruining your life, and I can help you. As I see it you have two choices: First, you can go to court with an attorney I know and if you get off, I can help you move out of the area because otherwise they will probably kill you; or second, you can keep on with the gang, continue on with the criminal life you are currently living, and probably spend the rest of your life behind bars. It's your choice, Bret. I hope you choose wisely."

It is quite dangerous to get oneself out of a gang affiliation. Sometimes not only the life of the teen is at risk, but the lives of their family members are endangered as well. After struggling with the idea of having to leave town and his family, Bret chose that option. He went to court and got 30 days of community service because his was a first-time offense. He and his mother met with Pastor Franklin, and Ida was advised that for Bret to be somewhat safe, he would have to move out of the area. Bret had been a "core" gang member, and as such, he had been very involved in gang activities and dependent on the gang for social and economic support. Ida was distraught. Pastor Franklin also told Ida that she and her family might be in danger, and counseled them to also move out of the area. Ida reluctantly agreed with that part of the plan. She wanted her daughters to be safe. Luckily, Pastor Franklin had connections in another state who assisted Ida with finding a new apartment, a new job, and registering her three children in school. Luckily, the gang to which Bret belonged was not national. Otherwise such an escape would not have been so safe due to the mobility of other gang members and their contacts in other cities.

Gang attire is not to be ignored. Owning articles that are beyond a teen's financial means is not to be ignored. Bret's situation ended happily because he was able to reverse his bad decision to join a gang early in his life. Had Bret's donning of colors been caught at the onset, he and his family might not have had to suffer the consequences of a bad teenage decision.

There are lots of guardians of teens who are unaware of their adolescent's involvement in gangs. While some might say these caregivers are uninvolved, there are many parents who have been as involved as they can be and are blindsided when they learn (usually through the legal system) their teen is a member of a gang. This is serious business. Your teen's life and future are at risk.

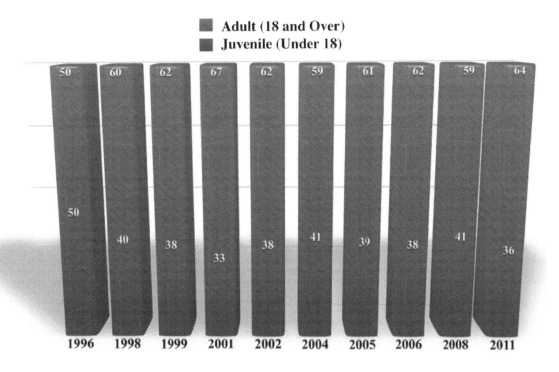

"National Youth Gang Survey Analysis." National Gang Center. Accessed July 24, 2016.
https://www.nationalgangcenter.gov/survey-analysis/demographics.

Attire Contract

Agreement	My Responsibilities	Consequences for Breaking Agreements
This contract is made to give you space to be yourself, as long as your choices are not dangerous to you or others.	Parents: If you notice some out-of-norm attire preferences, open communication about them with your teen. Teen: Advise your parents if you are attracted to a subculture and provide the reasons why. Explain what the subculture is about.	Parents: Being blindsided by your teen's involvement in possibly dangerous situations. Teen: Making decisions that could put your life at risk.
There is to be no gang involvement. Parents: Will report teen to law enforcement if they suspect teen is involved in gang activity. Will collect items of apparel/entertainment that were not given to teen by relatives, and turn them over to the police. Will detach from teen's legal problems that are a result of gang affiliation.	**Gang Involvement** Parents: Keep your teen out of dangerous affiliations. Call police, pastor, or counselor if you suspect your teen is involved in gang/criminal activity. Teen: Do not put your family's lives at risk because you like the "thug lifestyle" and easy money.	Parents: Enabling your teen's poor and risky choices by not stopping them. Teen: Legal problems in which your parents will not provide for your defense.
Although these are advertised as alcohol-free all-night dances, we parents realize that drug use is common. While living in the family home, teen will not attend raves. Any clothing suggestive of rave attire will be disposed of.	**Raves** Parents: Stay informed as to your teen's whereabouts and social plans. Check them out with other parents. Teen: Keep away from events where drug use is the communal norm.	Parents: Putting your teen at risk of drug overdose. Teen: If you attend a rave, your parent(s) will arrange for accompanying you to the next one. You may not ditch your parent(s) during the rave. A drug test will be given the next day.
In order to guide you away from extremes, if you find yourself attracted to this subculture, a family discussion must be held. It is to include your reasons for wanting to join a goth group. These reasons must be supported by parents. Otherwise, when you are self-supporting, joining this subculture is your choice.	**Goth** Parents: Monitor the extent of the "gothness." Remember, there is a part of this subculture that is extreme and does not foster balanced mental health. Teen: Do not allow this subculture to take over your life. Keep up your schoolwork and participate in other activities.	Parents: Your teen could become involved in the life-threatening extremes of this group. Teen: You will let this subculture define who you are—when you are so much more than that. Eccentric practices could begin to look normal.
If you are considering joining an emo subculture, you must present your parents with your reasoning. They will determine if they think this is a healthy affiliation for you.	**Emo** Parents: Familiarize yourselves with the pros and cons of this subculture. Weigh if your teen would benefit from it or not. Some teens find a way to express themselves through the emo subculture. Decide if that is a possibility for your teen. Teen: Emo is a lifestyle that you may outgrow. Be open to that possibility.	Parents: Members of the emo subculture often become depressed. This could happen to your teen if it is not monitored. Teen: Embracing the emo lifestyle to such a degree that you shut out all other possibilities.

Participation in Sports

High school can be such an exciting time because there is so much to discover! If your teen enjoys sports, they might find a great mentor in high school who will assist them in excelling. They could learn about many sports, or realize that they simply enjoy the exercise that comes along with participating in one sport. Usually basketball, baseball, softball, lacrosse, football, swimming, diving, field hockey, golf, tennis, wrestling, soccer, water polo, volleyball, cheerleading, gymnastics, and track are sports to consider. There are so many choices it might be difficult for your teen to decide what to try.

Here are some discussion ideas. Having conversations with your teen about their interest or lack of interest in high school sports could provide guidance and a way to alleviate confusion.

1. What sport(s) do you like the best?
2. It doesn't matter what your friends are doing, what sport do YOU like best?
3. No one can participate in every sport they like. After all, there is that matter of getting an education, too.
4. Is there some sport you haven't tried before that you would like to sign up for?
5. Express parental concerns about sports that are notorious for causing injury. Is there a particular sport in which you do not want your teen to participate? To get an idea of which

high school sports cause the most injuries, go to the National High School Sports-Related Injury Surveillance Study.[1]

6. Are you afraid of not succeeding? Not everyone is great at every sport. Some are not proficient in any sport. Parents must put this into perspective for their teen. Enjoyment has to be the goal. There is no reason why a student couldn't try many different sports over their four years in high school.

7. Instead of high school offerings is there any other "sport" that interests your teen such as martial arts, aerobics, working out at the gym, etc.

Why would it be beneficial for your teen to participate in a sport or in some type of exercise? Sports teach cooperation and competition. Playing a sport assists your adolescent in learning that with practice comes improvement. Sports help your teen learn to comply with sets of rules. They also learn that there are consequences for breaking the rules… rather like they learn from the contracts provided in this book.

Henry

Henry was entering his sophomore year of high school. Henry's mother and father had decided that Henry should focus on academics during his freshman year, but now that Henry was entering 10th grade, his father, who had been his high school's star quarterback, was encouraging Henry to try out for the football team. Henry, however, showed no interest. Like his mother, Henry was diminutive in stature and was convinced that football was not his game. He was interested in swimming. He was interested in art. His dad often said, "Henry must not be my son!"

After much cajoling from his dad, Henry agreed to try out for football. Because he was fast on his feet, he made the team, but Henry told his father he would rather try out for the swim team instead. Henry's father shared with Henry his fondest memories about how fun it was to be on the football team; he recalled some of his team's best victories and the parades that were held when his team won the state conference. Henry listened, but it was not his dream. Henry did play high school football for two years because it made his father happy. He spent much of his time on the bench and felt that every game was a disappointment to his dad because he was not a star.

Senior year, Henry left the football team and tried out for the swim team. He enjoyed his year with his team and became one of his school's swim stars. At college, Henry enjoyed four more years on the swim team.

We parents of teens must be careful not to try to relive our high school successes and dreams through our children. One of the greatest gifts we can give them is to honor their own interests and to foster their realizing their own dreams.

---

[1] http://www.ucdenver.edu/academics/colleges/PublicHealth/research/ResearchProjects/piper/projects/RIO/Documents/2012-13.pdf.

Fred

Fred was on the varsity football team his junior year of high school. He was 6'3" and recognized as a quarterback with enough talent that he could possibly be a professional. Fred's parents were avid football fans; they attended every game and held after-game parties for Fred and his teammates. Fred appeared to have it all—he was handsome, a great quarterback, and popular with his classmates. However, Fred had one problem: He didn't like to study because he was so focused on football, and felt too tired to do his homework after team practices. Fred had a GPA of C- the first half of his junior year.

Fred's parents were concerned that Fred would not have the necessary grades to make it into a college with a star football team. They were worried that because Fred was focused on football, he would not have the essential knowledge to achieve acceptable SAT scores. They put Fred's long-term needs in front of their own excitement about having the star quarterback as their son. Fred's parents decided to help him focus on his academics BEFORE he focused on football.

Fred's parents hated the idea that they might have to tell Fred that he was off the football team because of his low grades. Fred's coach joined with his parents in support of the contract, below. Fred did take advantage of his tutor and prep classes and was eventually accepted into a college with a great football team where, once again, he was the star quarterback.

Participating in Sports Contract

Agreements	My Responsibilities	Consequences for Breaking Agreements
During the hour between the end of classes and the beginning of football practice, a tutor will meet with you to review your homework and assist you in challenging subjects.	Teen: Work with tutor to complete assignments and to prep for tests.	Teen: Continuing to produce low scholastic achievements will diminish your college choices and jeopardize your ability to be a member of the football team.
Parent(s): Will pay for tutor up to 7 hours/week.	Parent(s): Pay for tutor.	Parent(s): Knowing you are not providing the scholastic help that could benefit your teen.
Parent(s): Research learning centers in your area that specialize in SAT prep. Teen: One day of the weekend for two hours, attend SAT prep classes.	Parent(s): Pay for prep classes. Teen: Take advantage of the SAT prep classes by actively addressing academic areas which are challenging for you.	Teen: Sometimes high SAT scores can somewhat offset GPAs. This is an opportunity to excel. If you choose not to, you will be limiting your college choices.
Teen: By the end of the second semester of junior year, have at least a B average.	Teen: To do your homework and study for tests so you can raise your grades.	Teen: If you are unable to maintain a 3.0 GPA, then you will take a leave of absence from the football team. Attending summer school to bring up your GPA.
Teen: If by the beginning of senior year, grades have not reached a 3.0 GPA, your membership in the football team will be terminated so you can focus on academics.	Teen: To raise my GPA so you can get into a college with a good football team.	Teen: Limiting your college choices and your opportunities to play college football. This is all up to you.

Taking Specialty Lessons

When we give our teens the gift of taking lessons to help them hone a special talent, or because they think it is fun, they also have obligations. Minimally, their responsibility is to show up for the lesson. Some lessons require no outside practice—like taking hip hop dancing at the gym. Others require practice—such as taking piano or guitar. So many caregivers provide their young adults with specialty lessons and then find they feel they are being taken advantage of because their teen doesn't enthusiastically participate, or even show up, for the lesson.

Contracts provide an agreement about how the teen can keep being provided specialty lessons. A contract allows for the parents to advise their young adult with knowledge about what is expected of them in order to keep participating in their lessons.

Taking Specialty Lessons Contract

Agreements	My Responsibilities	Consequences for Breaking Agreements
Parents: Will pay for ____ lessons for three months and at the end of that time, will consider renewal.	Parents: To pay the instructor on time. At the end of three months, discuss renewal with your teen. Teen: To attend all sessions unless ill or some other extenuating circumstance approved by parent.	Lessons will immediately end.
Practice—teen will practice the daily amount of time as advised by the instructor.	Make space in the daily schedule to practice. Keep track of my practice responsibilities.	Lessons will be ended.
	Nagging Parents: Will not nag, or remind teen about practicing. This is the total responsibility of the person who is receiving the lessons.	Teen: Will know that their caregiver broke this contract. This will lead to the young adult following their parent's role modeling of not respecting the rules. Your choice, parents.
Equipment such as an instrument, apparel, tennis racquet, golf clubs, etc.	Teen: To take care of the equipment necessary to take your lessons. Equipment will not be replaced if lost or damaged through lack of care. Parents: Responsible for paying for repair of normal wear and tear.	Loss of necessary equipment will necessitate suspension of lessons. Teen will pay for lost equipment through doing jobs at home, for neighbors, holiday and birthday money.
	Enjoyment Teen: Have fun taking these lessons.	If lessons become a drudge, both parties agree to end them.

The Challenging Student

It can be very challenging for parents when they have a student who just doesn't care about academics. Often, students get punished before anyone explores the possible reasons for the "turn-off" of learning. Is there a learning disability? Are the subjects too difficult? Does the student have an attention deficit? Is your child using drugs or drinking? Are there social problems at school? It is crucial to investigate and to discover why your young adult is not achieving in school.

This contract is for those students who are oppositional, those who don't want to follow the rules and guidelines of the norm, those who want to challenge structure. Parents must become smarter than their offspring. Parents MUST provide structure so their teen can grow past this difficult stage of testing authority to the extreme.

If we parents are to become wise guides for our kids, we cannot deviate from the rules of the contract. One deviation and we are teaching our teen that our contract is there, but we don't really enforce it or it is negotiable. So, KISS—Keep It Simple Somehow!

The critical idea behind this contract is that the teen is choosing to follow either the guidelines or he/she is selecting the consequences. It's all on them. There is no need for arguing or explaining. The contract that has been placed on the refrigerator for all to see is indisputable!

With an oppositional teen, a signature on the contract is invited, but not required. They don't have to agree, and that is OK. They are living in our house and while they are here, they must follow the rules and contribute to the good of the family community. *Whether they want to or not!*

As you view the contract on the next page, notice that the consequences for violation of agreements are meant to be short and related to the agreement. For example, if a student is 15 minutes late to three classes, five days in the week, that will total 3.75 hours! That's a lot of time. So, if the student wants to go to the movies over the weekend, and the movie starts at 1:00 P.M., the student has to arrive 3.75 hours late. Since that is impractical, the teen would not be able to attend the movie. The 3.75 hours would then be erased. Please remember, this is all the teen's choice.

In the beginning of structuring one's family around a contract, parents will have to be the guides until the teen is familiar with how the contract works. Reading a contract and actually understanding how it really works can be two different things to a teen. Review your contract with your teen. Ask if they have any questions. If not, you will still have to be the guide.

Be sure not to put too many things in this contract. It can be added to later. If grades are an issue, address them later. First, work on showing up for school and going to class on time, staying there during the school day, and turning in homework.

The job of feeding one's pet gives the teen a feeling of belonging to the family community—regardless of what they tell you.

Contract for House, School, and Privilege Structure

Agreement	My Responsibilities	Consequences for Breaking Agreements
Teen: By 5:00 P.M. each day, dog/cat is to be fed.	Teen: Feed the family pet on a daily basis unless other arrangements are made, IN WRITING, *before* the time when a change in this agreement is needed.	Teen: If teen chooses not to feed family pet on time, teen is then electing to lose TV that night. Or teen gets to eat dinner at the time he/she feeds the dog! For continuous infractions (more than one week), computer will be off limits until teen has one week of feeding family pet on time. No extenuating circumstances will be considered, such as a need to use computer for schoolwork. Teen can use a school computer for such.
Teen: Attend school between 8:00 A.M. and 3:00 P.M. Teen is not allowed to leave the school grounds.	Teen: Stay at school during the school day. Parents: Contact truancy officer if teen breaks agreement.	Teen: Will be selecting the consequences determined by the truancy officer and any laws pertaining to school attendance.
Teen: Is to arrive in his/her classes on time.	Parents: Contact student's teachers for a weekly report. Keep a running total of tardies. When a special event comes up, teen will arrive at the event at a time equal to the accumulated amount of time late to school. If the total amount of late time is more than the length of the event, then the event will be missed. Teen: Attend every class in a timely manner.	Parents: Even if it is the prom, if you don't enforce this agreement, your teen will not take seriously the importance of being on time to their responsibilities.
Teen: Study time is between 7:00 P.M. and 9:00 P.M. Monday through Friday. The use of cell phones, television, and social media is disallowed during this time.	Parents: Provide teen with a quiet study area. If none is available at home, drive your teen to the local library and stay with him/her. Teen: Leave cell phone with parents during study time.	Teen: If teen uses cell phone or social media during study time, cell phone will be removed from teen's possession for one day.
Teen: Complete homework on time and turn it in on time. If you are struggling with your assignments, ask for a tutor or for extra help at school.	**Homework** Teen: It is your JOB to attend school and to study to prepare yourself for a career of your choice. Homework is to be returned to teacher no later than the deadline. Parent: It is my job to provide you food, home, a quiet study area, and to assist you in reaching your goals.	Teen: If homework is not received by teacher prior to the deadline, teen is then electing to study between 7:00 P.M. and 9:00 P.M. on one day of the weekend.

CHAPTER 2

The Computer

Let's face it, it's necessary for our teens and young adults to have access to a computer. Sometimes families have just one computer that is shared by the family community. Other times, a teen/young adult is fortunate enough to have their own computer. In either situation, a contract is necessary.

In today's culture, the Web gives us access to so much information that we can find ourselves spending hours playing games, researching topics we never even thought of, engaging in social media, etc. The Internet can also provide dating opportunities, and sites relating to all kinds of porn. The Web provides pedophiles with myriad pathways for communicating with unsuspecting young people, whom they consider prey. For teens and young adults, safety and structure must be provided by their caregivers.

For some, the Web enables teens to isolate and avoid learning the social skills that are necessary for interpersonal relationships. Instead of looking someone in the eye and having a conversation or engaging in collaboration, or having to get through a conflictual problem, these isolative Internet users withdraw from anything personal, and develop "virtual friends." "Virtual friends" are those with whom we have no physical contact, but with whom we exchange written or photographic information. They are those phantoms who write us, and whom we never meet.

It is the responsibility of all guardians of our youth to provide structure and mentoring about the beneficial uses of the Web, as well as the inherent dangers that can come with its use. The establishment of a contract about the use of the computer and the allowable content that can be accessed will assist in providing our young adults with structure and values.

Let your young adult know that you will be blocking porn sites and checking on what sites have been accessed on the computer. One can seek advice about how to do this on your computer from a friend or a professional at somewhere like Best Buy or Office Depot.

Provided below are several samples of computer contracts. Each is tailored to a specific situation. For the family that is sharing one computer, it is important that the adults incorporate the guidelines for their own computer use into the contract. This provides a foundation for an environment of cooperation and equanimity. If caregivers say, or imply, that they are exempt from limiting their computer use for the good of the community, why should the other family members not adopt the same attitude? Role modeling the spirit of sharing and demonstrating respect for the rights of others helps families bond and develop closer ties. Change the contract to fit the needs of your family. If you change the Consequences for Breaking Agreements section, be sure to have those consequences have to do with computer use, and not anything else.

In the following contract, a family of four has one computer. In an effort to provide use of the computer to all family members in a fair and equitable way, they established these agreements.

Contract for a Family With One Computer and a Stay-at-Home Family Member

Agreement	My Responsibilities	Consequences for Breaking Agreements
Mom/partner/girlfriend, etc.: Will have use of the computer for two hours during the day. Mom will take her time during the hours that other family members are at school or at their jobs. On weekends, Mom will have use of the computer when no one else is using it—not to exceed two hours a day.	Be honest about the time spent on the computer.	Because during the week Mom will be using the computer when no one is home, Mom agrees to abide by her two-hour limit. Consequences for not honoring this part of the contract are that Mom knows she is being dishonest with her family.
Dad/partner/boyfriend, etc.: Will have use of computer for two hours after other family members have completed their allotted time.	Time yourself and comply with this contract.	Your family will know if you are not adhering to the terms of this contract, and if you don't respect this contract, why should anyone else? In effect, the contract will become null and void if you don't respect it.
Sibling 1: Computer use from 7 P.M.–8 P.M. for homework use only and from 9 P.M.–10 P.M. for homework use and social media interaction once homework is completed.	Monitor your computer use in an honest way by setting a timer. Willingly turn over computer to the person next in line. Save all work so that it will not be lost. Attend to other homework during break from computer.	Violation will result in the loss of computer time in 30-minute increments. Violation are things such as arguing, not leaving the computer when time is up, or using inappropriate language.
Sibling 2: Computer from 8 P.M.–9 P.M. for homework use only; from 10 P.M.–11 P.M. for homework and social media interaction once homework is completed.	Monitor my computer use in an honest way by setting a timer. Willingly turn over computer to the person next in line. Save any work so that it will not be lost. Attend to other homework during break from computer.	Violation will result in the loss of computer time in 30-minute increments. Violation are things such as arguing, not leaving the computer when time is up, or using inappropriate language.
	Weekend Use On each weekend day, computer may be used for two hours. If homework is done, the computer can be used for video games, and siblings may combine time.	Any arguing, swearing, or disagreements about computer use will result in loss of computer time in 30-minute increments.

For the family in which the teens have their own computer, it is very important for caregivers to set limits on its use. Sometimes, teens can be required to bring their laptop to the dining room table to do their homework. More responsible young adults could be given the privilege of unmonitored use in their bedrooms. All of this will depend on the maturity, reliability, and motivation of the person using the computer.

Turned over to their own devices, some teens will play video games during the time allotted for homework and as a fill-in for having one-on-one interaction with others. In fact, the latest research shows that by the time the average teen reaches 21, they will have spent about 10,000 hours playing video games.[2] There is also a great deal of new evidence that is showing that video gaming can negatively affect brain function.

The research about how video gaming affects one's brain is in its infancy, and there is much controversy about the positive and negative findings. Brain research initially found that gamers gained more efficient attention abilities and increased their motor skills from playing their video games.[3] Now, new research has discovered that those who spend a great deal of time playing video games (six hours per week) have an increased risk of neurological disorders such as Alzheimer's.[4,5] Those who played violent video games can become more prone to aggressive behavior and became desensitized to violence.[6] Whatever the final scientific results are regarding how gaming affects the developing and mature brain, right now there is solid concern about the addictive qualities of gaming.

Today, video gaming is considered an impulse control disorder that is very similar to pathological gambling.[7] Some of the signs of having a video gaming disorder are: feelings of restlessness and/or irritability when unable to play, preoccupation with thoughts of previous online activity or anticipation of the next online session, lying to friends or family members regarding the amount of time spent playing, isolation from others in order to spend more time gaming, fatigue, migraines due to intense concentration or eye strain, carpal tunnel syndrome caused by the overuse of a controller or computer mouse, and lack of attention to personal hygiene.

While not yet formally diagnosed, Internet gaming disorder is being considered for future study and possible addition to the *Diagnostic and Statistical Manual of Mental Disorders*. At this time, what we know is that video gaming can become an addiction, and early trials show that treating it with a medication called bupropion (Wellbutrin), which is used as an antidepressant and for smoking cessation, can change the brain's chemistry and help it to decrease cravings for video game play.[8]

In today's culture, it seems like just about all teens play some video games. While we accept that, it is extremely important that we parents teach our young adults how to have responsible game time.

---

[2] *"New Light on Impact of Video Gaming on the Brain,"* Science Daily, *May, 19, 2015.*

[3] *C. Shawn Green and Aaron R. Seitz. "The Impacts of Video Games on Cognition (and How the Government Can Guide the Industry)."* Policy Insights from the Behavioral and Brain Sciences *2015, Vol. 2(1) 101-110.*

[4] *Greg L. West, Brandi Lee Drisdelle, Kyoko Konishi, Jonathan Jackson, Pierre Jolicoeur, Veronique D. Bohbot. "Habitual action video game playing is associated with caudate nucleus-dependent navigational strategies."* Proceedings of the Royal Society B, *May 2015.*

[5] *Craig A. Anderson et al. "Violent Video Game Effects on Aggression, Empathy, and Prosocial Behavior in Eastern and Western Countries: A Meta-Analytic Review."* Psychological Bulletin *2010, Vol. 136, No. 2, 151–173.*

[6] *Hank Pellissier. "Your Child's Brain on Technology: Video Games." www.greatschools.org. February 26, 2016.*

[7] *"Video Games Addiction." Illinois Institute for Addiction Recovery. www.addictionrecov.org/Addictions/?AID=45.*

[8] *Romeo Vitelli, PhD. "Are Video Games Addictive?"* Psychology Today, *August 19, 2013.*

Allowing a teen to play extended hours of video games only serves to teach them that isolation is preferable and more exciting than socializing one on one. Video gaming may be a great "babysitter" because you know where your teen and his/her friends are and what they are doing, but resist the temptation to allow gaming for more than two hours/day. One might also limit gaming to the weekends so that young adults are not distracted from their homework and get enough sleep.

Social networking agreements are in this chapter. Suffice it to say that such a contract is necessary whenever teens/young adults have use of a computer. If desired, parents can incorporate guidelines for social networking into the contract; however, a separate agreement regarding parental structure of teen use of social networks provides clarity for that one topic.

It is a privilege to have one's own computer. Often such use is taken for granted or is considered a personal "right." The attitude with which the use of a computer is received is dependent on one's parents/caregivers. When parents treat their computer as a great privilege, and something to really be appreciated and cared for, their attitude is usually picked up by their teens.

If you have a college student who will be taking their computer to school with them, it will be difficult to have a meaningful agreement that is enforceable. However, a contract regarding risk, loss, and maintenance is beneficial because it delineates who has what responsibility regarding the computer. It is important to address situations that could occur regarding loss of the computer due to theft, lending it to a friend, damage due to carelessness, etc. Who is going to pay for the replacement? Who is going to deal with the friend who borrowed it and won't return it? If parents rescue young adults from the natural consequences of their bad decisions, the parents are teaching the young adult that they will be rescued, and there really no consequences for carelessness.

It is tempting to rescue. It is more respectful to ask your young adult just what they think the options might be for solving a computer issue. LISTEN. Support them in figuring out the answer. That is the way they learn!

Contract for the Family that Has Individual Computers

Agreements	My Responsibilities	Consequences for Breaking Agreements
Teen: During the week, my computer will be used for homework and social networking.	Teen: Limit myself to no more than one hour per weekday night for engaging in social networking. Set a time for doing that, and let my caregivers know the hour I have selected.	Teen: For one day, the inability to use my computer for the one hour designated for social networking.
Teen: Up to two hours per weekend day can be dedicated to playing video games on my computer if my homework is done first.	Teen: Set a timer. Keep track of my time.	Teen: Going over the two-hour gaming time will result in losing the video gaming time on the next weekend day.
Teen and parents: The holder of the computer has the responsibility to keep it safe from theft and damage.	Teen and parents: If the computer leaves the house and something happens to it, such as it is stolen or damaged, it will be the responsibility of the holder of the computer to pay for replacement or repairs.	Teen and parents: Having no computer until a new one can be purchased by the holder of the computer that was lost, stolen, or damaged. This will cause resentments if the computer is not immediately replaced.
For the computer that mainly stays at home, repairs for malfunction will be paid for by the parents.	Parents: Pay for repairs and maintenance of your teen's computer. Teen: Inform caregivers if there is a problem with the computer in a timely manner.	Parents: If you decide to break this agreement, you are teaching your teen that it is OK to ignore the terms of this contract and thus, you will have rendered this contract null and void through no fault of the teen's. Breaking of contracts by parents has far-reaching negative ramifications.
Parents: Will pay for any training/lessons that student deems necessary to enable him/her to be more efficient on the computer.	Teen: Advise caregivers of the need for training. Investigate the cost and location of the training. Parents: Set a limit on the price you will be willing to pay for computer training. Make an agreement about how your teen will get transportation for the training.	Teen: Not acquiring advanced computer skills.
Teen: Will pay for necessary maintenance.	Parents: Set up a plan with young adult about timing for maintenance.	Increased costs for parents to repair problems that could have been prevented through annual maintenance.

All these computer contracts are great, but what if parents are out working and not at home to enforce them? This can pose a real problem. Every contract has to be enforceable! If it isn't, it's just a waste of paper and effort. Investigate methods to monitor computer use. There is software for monitoring the Internet, chats, text messages, Facebook, cell phones, etc. Guardians must empower themselves to be in control of computer use; otherwise, who knows in what danger a teen might unwittingly put themselves?

If is very challenging for working parents to provide structure for their teen during the day—and during the day is just the time they need it! Perhaps relatives or extended family can be around to make sure contracts are respected. Make arrangements for your young adult to have some accountability between when school ends and when a caregiver returns home from work. Have them call you when they start to use their computer. This can be part of your contract.

Computer Use Contract: Working Parents

Agreements	My Responsibilities	Consequences for Breaking Agreements
Parents: Installing a monitoring device on your computer to help in keeping you safe. It will assist you in putting structure in your life.	Parents: Research, pay for and install software for monitoring computer use. Keep teen safe from stalkers and pedophiles. Help provide structure between the end of school and when parents come home from work.	Parents: Have elected to put teen at risk for dangerous situations and inability to self-structure. By acknowledging this computer contract, teens are also advised that parents did not keep them safe or provide guidelines for structure.
Teen: Return from school at 3:30.	Have a snack if desired. It will be in the (location). Rest for half an hour. Begin homework for an hour and may use computer during this time.	If teen doesn't comply, he/she has elected forfeiting the reward. For each infraction thereafter, there will be a loss of social networking time for that day.
Parents: Will monitor computer use. A reward will be given at the end of each week for compliance.	Parents: Will provide a meaningful reward each week. It will be a surprise.	It is the parent's responsibility to provide a reward each week. Consequence for not following through is that your teen will know you did not comply with this contract, and that being the case, why should he/she/they? Respect for this contract is up to the parents.
Between 5 P.M. and 5:30 P.M. social media may be used.	Parents: Are using a monitor to help young adult comply with this contract.	Loss of computer for one day. No negotiation. No extenuating circumstances. The use of the computer is dependent upon compliance with this contract.
Parents: Will check the monitors each evening.	Parents: To make sure there are no excuses for not following through with this.	Your young adult will not take this contract seriously and because you don't check, they will think non-compliance will slide by you. It is also unfair to only monitor occasionally. Consequences must be realized on the day this contract is violated, otherwise they seem irrelevant to a teen.

Strangers on the Internet

The statistics are alarming! According to the *Journal of Adolescent Health* 47 (November 2010), 65% of online sex offenders used the victim's social networking sites to gain information about them. While only 18% of teens use chatrooms, the majority of Internet-initiated sex crimes against youth begin in chatrooms. Over half of teens solicited online were asked to send a photo; 27% of the pictures were sexually oriented in nature. One in seven minors has received a sexual solicitation online. The majority of victims of Internet-initiated sex crimes were between 13 and 15 years old. Fourteen percent of 10th–12th graders have accepted an invitation to meet an online stranger in person.

With knowledge of these statistics, making a contract with your teen about Internet use becomes critical. Establishing guidelines and enforcing them in a contract turns into a life-and-death matter. Please have a discussion about Internet use with your teen and address the risks of corresponding with strangers and posting personal information on their social media sites.

What is your teen looking at on the Internet? YouTube shows demonstrations of just about anything, including videos about teen suffocation techniques, sex, adolescents tripping on drugs, and information about drugs that defy standard urine tests. Compared to their parents, most teens are experts when it comes to the computer. They know how to block certain content from the "prying eyes" of their guardians. It might be a good idea to have your teen provide you with the user names and passwords of their accounts so you can monitor more closely. If you monitor one child, you need to monitor all of them. Remember, teens are very creative and skilled when it comes to getting around monitoring devices. They know how to clear browser history. Open communication is the best way to help your teen be safe on the Internet.

Computer Use Contract: Strangers on the Internet and Inappropriate "Research"

Agreements	My Responsibilities	Consequences for Breaking Agreements
Teen: Will not respond to people on the Internet who you do not know. Parent(s): Will be monitoring your Internet use to protect you from possibly dangerous people. We love you and want to keep you safe.	Teen: Protect myself from strangers who could harm me. Parent(s): Protect your teen from strangers on the Internet.	Teen: Loss of your social media sites for two months. Parent(s): If you do not monitor your teen's Internet use, you could be putting their safety at risk.
Teen: Will login to your social network accounts and show them to your parents. Provide parents with user names and passwords. Parent(s): Schedule this event in your calendar.	**Once a Month** Teen: Be honest and forthcoming with your parents about what your social media accounts are. Add friends and family members to your "Friend" circle. Parents: Enlist friends and family members to help you monitor.	Teen: Loss of your social media sites for two months. Parent(s): Not knowing what your teen is doing online.
Parent(s): Will install a monitoring application to alert them if there is something they should be aware of. This is for all family members under the age of 18.	Parent(s): Research monitoring options so that you can be alerted more often than the once a month parent/teen Internet check.	Parent(s): You will not know what your teen is looking at on the Web and whom they are in contact with.
Teen: Will alert parents if contacted by strangers and show parents the communication.	Teen: Keep yourself safe from possible online predators. Parent(s): Assist your teen in keeping himself/herself safe from strangers on the Internet by following through with monitoring your teen's computer.	Teen: Possibly putting your life at risk. Not informing your parents indicates lack of good judgment. Parents will monitor your computer daily for one month. Parent(s): No follow through shows your teen that you are not as protective as you say you are. They will then question your credibility.
Parent(s): It is our responsibility to guide you into behaviors that will benefit your life. Researching ways people harm themselves is off limits. Teen: If you don't know if your parents would approve of a research topic, ask them.	**Inappropriate "Research"** Parents(s): Address this topic as necessary. It may be necessary to name the topics that are not going to benefit your teen's life. You will have to gauge this. Teen: If you are curious about something that you know your parents won't approve, ask them to help you research it anyway.	Teen: Will have to use their computer in a family area for the next six months. Continued violation will result in loss of your computer except for homework assignments which will be done in a family area and monitored by your parents. Loss of cell phone account for three months.

Monitoring the Internet

Don't think your teens are brilliant about hiding their Internet adventures from you? Here's the 2012 research from CNN on the topic of just how our teens outsmart us. Their study revealed that 70% of teens hide their online behavior from their parents. The list CNN compiled shows the percentage of teens who said they engaged in hiding their Internet searches from their parents and how they did it:

1. Clear browser history (53%)
2. Close/minimize browser when parent walked in (46%)
3. Hide or delete IMs or videos (34%)
4. Lie or omit details about online activities (23%)
5. Use a computer your parents don't check (23%)
6. Use an Internet-enabled mobile device (21%)
7. Use privacy settings to make certain content viewable only by friends (20%)
8. Use private browsing modes (20%)
9. Create private email address unknown to parents (15%)
10. Create duplicate/fake social network profiles (9%)

Are you feeling that you will never win the monitoring battle? Knowledge is power. After reading the above information just think about how much more informed you are now than you were before you had these statistics. Are you uncertain about how to find the history of what has been "researched" on the Internet? Here are some tips:

Chrome: Clicking Ctrl-H will bring up the History menu.
Internet Explorer: Find the "Favorites" menu. Select "History." There you will find a listing that can be sorted by date, site name, and by sites visited most often or most frequently.
Safari: Find the "History" menu. Select "Show All History." To search further back, go to Safari's menu, select "Preferences," and in "General Preferences" look for "Remove History Items" and select a time frame.
Firefox: Select the "History" menu and then select "Show All History."
uKnowKids.com is a good resource to alerting parents to inappropriate photos and language in their social networking.
Google will provide you with a vast amount of choices and information about contacts for monitoring your teen's Internet activities.

Ideas for Inappropriate "Research"

In my years of practice, I often think I have heard every topic our creative teens can up with to investigate. Each time I begin to think that thought, I am proven wrong! There is always something new that I would never have thought of in a million years. I'm sure you will be able to add to this list. Have fun with it instead of becoming aghast at what pops into your teen's mind. If your teen is interested in some topic that is abhorrent to you, research it with them anyway. It fosters teen/parent bonding and at the very least, you will know what interests your teen!

- How to grow marijuana in your garage
- Growing marijuana in your room
- Edibles (food containing marijuana)
- Making your own alcohol
- How to make your pupils look normal after drug use
- Getting over on a drug test
- High-risk car games
- What is sexting all about
- Birth control
- Abortion
- How to give yourself an abortion
- Sexually transmitted diseases
- Teen pregnancy
- How to lose weight by vomiting
- Diets
- Diet pills
- Ways to win a physical fight
- Gangs
- Pornography
- Different sexual positions
- Being bisexual, transsexual, homosexual, transgender
- Sexual preference issues
- Emo
- Suicide and ways to do it
- Research about different drugs
- How to get high
- Recipe for making one's own drugs by using cough syrup
- Fashion
- Relationship issues: How to get the boy; how to flirt; does he/she like me?

- Tongue, nipple, genital piercings
- Tattoos

There are many more interests teens have. Be curious with your teen. There will be less secrecy as a result.

The graph below shows how making one's teens aware of Internet dangers positively influences them to not divulge personal information.

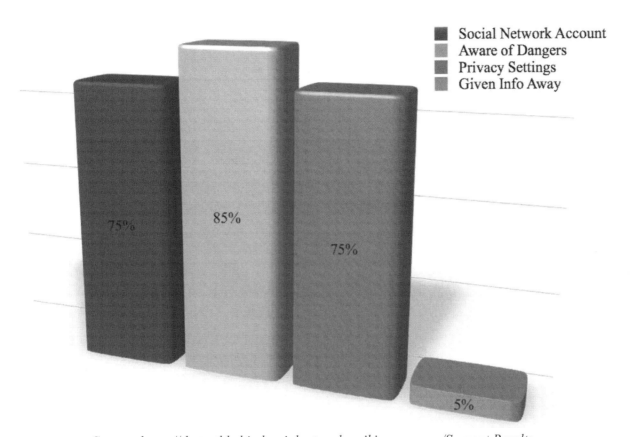

Source: https://thetruthbehindsocialnetworks.wikispaces.com/Survey+Results

Cyberbullying

This has become a huge media topic. How many news stories have we had about teen suicide due to harassment, gossip, and character assassination on the Internet? Forty-three percent of teens have been victims of cyberbullying in the last year! Cyberbullying involves using cell phones and the Internet via social media to harass or intimidate another person. There are many ways to communicate such mean-spiritedness. Some of the most common methods involve spreading malicious rumors online or through texts, posting daunting or threatening messages on Facebook or other social networking sites, sending demeaning emails or texts, pretending to be someone else online to hurt another person, and attaching degrading captions to unflattering photographs of the victim and posting them on the Web. Beware of Snapchat, which allows one to send short videos and images to people which "delete" instantly after the receiver views them.

Have you ever read *Lord of the Flies*? Being a victim of cyberbullying reminds me of how Piggy must have felt as he was isolated from his peers and left to die on his own. Being singled out by one's peer group as the "identified weirdo," the "one with no redeeming characteristics," can lead to teen depression, anxiety, isolation, and suicide. Remember, things posted on the Internet NEVER disappear.

Why do teens cyberbully? Many think it's a joke. They think it's funny. Additionally, most teens believe that everyone cyberbullies, so why shouldn't they?

All of us adults have a duty to protect the younger generation from such humiliating and shaming experiences. Discuss this with your teen. Develop a safety contract. It provides your loved one with a loving plan with which to safeguard him/herself. Most teens would not get involved with cyberbullying. If you find your teen has joined a group of bullies, he/she needs more guidance and structure. A contract is in order.

Cyberbullying Contract

Agreements	My Responsibilities	Consequences for Breaking Agreements
Teen: No texting or posting of mean messages or photos on the Internet. Caregiver: With your teen's knowledge, monitor texts, emails, and social networks.	Teen: Even if you don't like someone, you may not disrespect them via text, email or social networks. Caregiver: Monitor often. Have discussions about appropriate ways to interact or not interact with people who are not liked by your teen.	Teen: Demeaning someone on the Internet is serious. If you decide to do this, you will lose your cell phone and computer privileges for two months. Caregiver: Cyberbullying can ruin another teen's life. The consequences of not knowing what your teen is doing on the Internet will fall on both the teen and you.
Teen: Report to your caregiver if you are the victim of cyberbullying. Caregiver: Check in with your teen if he/she is receiving mean texts or degrading emails or comments on their social networking pages.	Teen: While it might be embarrassing to tell your caregiver that you are being called names and stories are being made up about you, it is your responsibility to provide this information so your caregiver can provide you with safety. Caregiver: Address your teen's report. Become an investigator to get the facts. Get copies of texts, emails, and postings.	Teen: If you don't seek support, you will go this alone, and that is not necessary. Asking for help is a courageous act. Do it. Caregiver: You might not find out that your teen is being cyberbullied if you don't monitor their Internet sites.
Teen: Do you fear that if you seek help, your bullies will become more intimidating? Ask the bully to stop. Seek help if that doesn't solve the issue. If you don't seek help, all you are doing is empowering the people who are hurting you. Tell someone. If you don't, nothing will change.	**"Don't Rat"** **(that outdated teen guideline)** Teen: Tell your caregiver who is bullying you. Block communication with them. Discuss the bullying with your friends. Consider getting offline and changing your phone number. Caregiver: With your teen, create a safety plan. Contact the school. Plan with school administrators what needs to be done. YOU are the only one that can protect your teen.	Teen: If you don't take steps to end the bullying, you will continue to feel hurt, scared and angry. The bullying will get worse. Caregiver: If you do nothing, your teen will be all alone in a battle he/she is ill prepared to handle. You will watch their angst and be reminded that you didn't take action to provide safety.
Teen: Know that you cannot handle this yourself. If you could, you would have done so by now.	Teen: Know that some caregivers will encourage you to deal with a bullying situation by taking physical action. Your responsibility is to deal with your bully through appropriate channels. Talk with your school counselor.	Teen: The bullying will continue. Caregiver: You miss an opportunity to bond with your teen by joining with them in finding avenues through which the bullying will be forced to stop.
Teen: Cyberbullying is often an extension of bullying that is going on at school. If this is the case, tell your caregiver.	Teen: Report bullying at school to your counselor, principal, dean. Caregiver: Listen to your teen tell you about their experience.	Teen and Caregiver: If you don't join together to end the bullying, it will continue.

CHAPTER 3

Let's Party: The High School Coming-of-Age Rituals

What are your values regarding high school "partying"? And what does the word "party" mean to most teens? The hundreds of teens that I have had the privilege of treating have taught me that "party" means to drink/use and get drunk/high. That is how they define it. When I inquire if there might be another definition, I am looked at as if I was some ancient fossil from another world who is asking questions in a different language. "Party" needs to be redefined! Why have we adults allowed teens to place a new meaning on the word "party" so that it is now a code for "Let's get together and become so drunk/high that we lose our ability to function"?

Given the teen definition of "party," we guardians of teens must protect them from putting themselves at risk of making bad decisions with long-range consequences. If we allow them to "party" at our home, the message we are giving is, "I don't care if you engage in underage drinking or experimenting." This attitude, by the way, gives covert permission to one's teen to repeatedly use alcohol and drugs. Many parents believe that their high school teens will drink and perhaps try marijuana anyway, so he/she might as well do it at home. Be clear about what your values are, and what you expect from your teen. Remember, most teenage use of mind-altering chemicals is done with the intent to get drunk/high. Not only can this be life-threatening, but many teens become addicted after thinking they are engaging in recreational use. Educate your teens about the risks of addiction to mind-altering chemicals. You might even take them to an AA (Alcoholics Anonymous) or NA (Narcotics Anonymous) meeting to let them see what their future could be. (If this is a big issue for you, please consider reading my book *Let's Make a Contract: Getting Your Teen Through Substance Abuse* for more information.)

Most teens want to be one of "the group." They want to have friends to "do stuff with." Note how vague this is. Even they can't define what these ideas mean. Peer groups have great influence over our teenagers and it is important to know what "group" your teen has selected, and what it does in its spare time. If the group pastime isn't one that would be acceptable to most of us caregivers, then there will be an element of secrecy about the, who, what, where, when, and why of group gatherings. In an effort to divert your attention away from group get-togethers, your teen will play on the generation-gap accusation of "you don't understand" and "everyone does it." In response, we, who are regarded as being dull, out of touch with current trends, and rigidly conventional, will feel guilty. Don't allow yourself to be manipulated by guilt-inducing accusations of being a "mean," "uncaring," and "nosey" parent. Teens test us, and if any of their intimidating techniques work to influence the reduction of parental involvement and the bending of guidelines and consequences, these will be used again and again. It will develop into a power struggle. You will become exhausted, frustrated, and angry. But more importantly, YOU won't win!

So, what if we circumvent the power struggle? If we become "smarter" than our teens, we might be able to guide them in ways that will help them establish a more engaging lifestyle. Have gatherings! Make them fun! Go have picnics, play baseball, take your teen and her friends to learn about various occupations or how to make items of interest to them. Teach them to play poker, chess, and other board games. Learn how to fish, or fly a kite. Arrange for a group of your teen's pals to volunteer at the local SPCA. Be creative. The more enthusiastic we parents can be about life, the more our teens will be interested in activities that will benefit them. Have a party! Give it a different definition than it currently holds for teens—getting drunk and high. Ask your teen what "having fun" looks like to them.

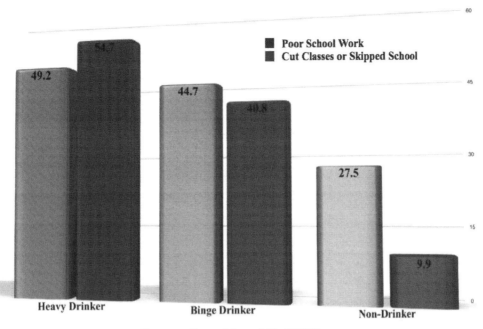

Source: Greenblatt, J.C. (2000)

Let's Party Contract: No Use of Drugs/Alcohol at Home

Agreements	My Responsibilities	Consequences for Breaking Agreements
Parents: We are proud that you are now in high school. We will do everything we can to be supportive so that you can succeed. We also want you to have fun.	Parents: Find out your teen's goals and interests. Have discussions about this. Teens have goals and interests that sometimes change weekly. Go with their "flow." DON'T say, "Last week you said you wanted to…" Stay in THEIR present.	Parents: You can't encourage or support what you don't know, and without parental interest, teens often find themselves trying to parent and entertain themselves—an impossible task.
Parents: We would like to know your friends and include them in some of our activities. Teen: Get permission to invite some of your pals over for family events.	Parents: Organize outings and ask your teen if he/she would like to bring one or two friends along. Teen: Have more fun! Bring a friend!	Parents: You might find your teen spending more time with the families of his/her friends.
Teen: Would you like to have a party at your home? Ask your parents. Parents: Be open to your teen's request to host a party. Select a party theme. "Come Have a Hot Dog." "Pizza Night." "Swim and Tan." "Skateboard and Eat." "Come for Horror Movie Night!" "Football Night." "Team Snowball Fights." Have fun with this.	Teen: You need to have input in party planning so your parents don't select a "corny" idea for a gathering of your friends. Remember, your parents probably don't know what is "kewl" to you. Parents: It is often easier to select an activity first and then plan the party around that.	Teen: You give up an opportunity to have fun with your pals, You miss out on congregating with your friends. Parents: You miss the chance to get to know your teen's friends and having fun with them.
	In and Out	
We will be monitoring if guests are going in and out of your activity. This usually indicates that there is another pastime going on outside our event. Guests could be asked to leave if they decide to participate in some behavior that takes them away from participating in our gathering.	Parents: Monitor the behavior of your guests. Some visitors enjoy leaving a gathering, going outside, smoking pot/drinking alcohol, and returning to an event, drunk or high. Your teen needs to know from you that this is not acceptable at your party. Teen: Advise your friends that your parents don't allow underage substance use.	Parents: If you give one substance user a "pass," and let him/her stay at your house under the influence, you are negating your own "no substance use by underage guests" value system. This will confuse your teen and give him a reason to argue with you because you did not enforce this agreement.
Drugs/Alcohol: Under no circumstances will teen or his/her friends be allowed to drink or use drugs in or around our home. If we feel one of your pals comes to our home under the influence, we will call his/her parents to come get them and take them home.	Parents: Protect any teen guest at your home from an overdose or from participating in underage substance use. Check out the laws in your state regarding the financial/legal consequences for parents who serve or allow underage people to drink/use at their home. Teen: Comply with the family values regarding underage use of mind-altering substances.	Parents: In many states, parents are held legally responsible for providing or allowing underage people to use alcohol/drugs. The risk is YOURS. Teen: By allowing your friend(s) to drink/use drugs at your house, you could be setting your parents up for severe legal and financial consequences.

Attending the Prom

There is usually much excitement around attending a junior or senior prom, a type of "rite of passage." What will I wear? How much does it cost? What does it include? Will we celebrate by having sex? Who has the alcohol/pot? Are we going to dinner? Do I have a date? Do I want a date? Do I even want to go? Will someone ask me to be their date?

It will be necessary to set guidelines, know what the plans are and whom your teen will be with, and to contact any parents who are reportedly having an after-party. With any topic that is not addressed, it is possible that your teen will be left to his/her own judgment. Only you, the guardian, will be able to decide if this is a good idea or not. One way to monitor your teen's prom is to volunteer to be a chaperone. Often the teen hates this idea, but it can turn out to be great fun for the parents. If you are on the "Prom Committee," you will have a say as to what goes on at the prom: Can students leave the event and then return? What happens to those who drink/smoke at the prom? What would be a fun theme? You can meet many students by running a poll about theme options. Get involved.

Contract for Attending the Prom

Agreements	My Responsibilities	Consequences for Breaking Agreements
Teen: Have fun. Guardian(s): Make this an exciting time for your teen. Participate, volunteer, paint props, cook—honor your teen's special day.	Teen: Think about what would make this night memorable and really fun. Tell your guardian. Guardian(s): Be receptive to your teen's feedback about what you could do to help make this evening extra special. If the response from your teen is "I don't know," then do something on your own. After all, you gave your teen a chance.	Teen: If you don't take the opportunity to say what would make the prom very fun for you, then you don't get to complain about anything because you opted not to participate in the planning. Guardian(s): If you nag your teen for feedback, you will shut down the conversation.
Teen: Prom is over at midnight. You are to be home by 12:45 (if you have a date) or 12:30 if you chose to not have a date. Your guardian is going to wait up for you.	**Curfew** Teen: Take your date home (if you choose to have one) and get home yourself on time. If you are being taken home by your date, honor his/her curfew. Guardian(s): Wait up for your teen or set your alarm for the curfew time.	Teen: Being awakened at 8:00 A.M. to go exercise, do household chores, and walk the dog for the next three hours. Your guardian will accompany you. Don't want to comply? See below. Guardian(s): If you don't respect this curfew agreement, why would your teen respect the next one?
Dinner: 6:00–7:30 Where: Transportation: Who pays: Dance: 8:00–midnight No leaving and returning to the prom. No alcohol/drug use.	**The Event Schedule** Teen: Stay on schedule and have fun at the prom. Guardian(s): Depending on your financial situation, assist your teen with prom expenses, provide transportation, support your teen's needs. Have the money discussion as you help plan for their big day.	Teen: You could ruin your own prom event. If you decide to use alcohol/drugs, you will attend five AA or NA meetings and be accompanied by your guardian. Guardian(s): Most teens don't have the financial ability to pay for some or maybe all prom expenses. Your teen will feel alone and unsupported if you don't at least volunteer your time.
Teen: Advise your parent if you need a tux, prom dress, flowers, etc. Guardian(s): There are many different ways to provide this: rent a dress/tux, make a dress, buy a new dress, cut flowers from your yard, learn how to make a corsage.	**Attire** Teen: Tell your guardian what you will need to wear to the prom at least one month in advance. Guardian(s): Create a budget. Discuss options.	Teen: If you wait until the last minute to discuss what to wear, you probably will not get the attire you need. Guardian(s): If you don't set your teen up for success by creating a contract, they will feel that they have a caregiver that isn't interested in them.
Teen: Agrees to comply with this contract. Guardian: Agrees to enforce this contract.	**Compliance** Teen: If I choose to not keep the above agreements, I acknowledge that I am selecting the consequences and will comply with them.	Teen: If you decide not to comply with any part of this contract, there will be loss of attending/participating in the next school sporting event (no matter what it is), loss of driving privileges for the next three weeks, loss of cell phone for the next three weeks, loss of computer time at home except for required school assignments. Computer will be moved to a public place.

More About Attending the Prom

Here's the prom formula—it's really very simple:

When is the event?
Where is the event?
How much will it cost? Who pays?
What will you wear?

How will you get there and home again?
Come home on time.
No drugs/alcohol use.

Have fun.

Prom Suggestions for Those in Recovery

Prom has a reputation for teen drinking and drug use, crimes, and accidents. There are some teens who are trying to overcome their past involvement with such activities. These are the teens in treatment for drug/alcohol abuse. They deserve our respect! Their job is to stay sober, and resist peer pressure. This is a Herculean task for high school students. They often feel like outcasts from the herd. They know that they must be mindful about their behavior. Every day, they are struggling to resist cravings for addictive substances. Their prom night is about more than the date, the meal, and the dance. It is about how to stay sober at an event that has the notorious reputation of having attendees who get drunk or high in celebration of moving on to a new stage of life. For those in recovery from substance addiction, they cannot participate in the "total" experience because sobriety has to be their first and foremost concern. Relapse can be a very serious problem. It will be necessary to help prepare for how your teen will get through the prom without relapsing. Much of this preplanning has to be your teen's. In the end, we guardians of teens cannot actually do very much about our loved one's choices when they are away from home. Having a contract may foster your teen's decision making.

Helpful Hints

1. For those teens in recovery during special events at school, focus on people who are NOT drinking/using as opposed to paying attention to those who are drunk or high.

2. Advise your date that you do not drink or use. Find out if he/she does. It is probably wise to date peers who don't consider getting drunk or high as a priority pastime.

3. Establish an accountability tree—that is, make a list of people you are going to contact before, during, and after the event to help center you in your recovery. Call them. If you don't call, give them permission to report to your guardian(s), and provide them with their phone number.

4. It may appear that your old using pals are having the best time of all. Remember, they are actually only acting stupid, while hurting their brains and bodies with drugs/alcohol. Recall the many instances in the news about teens dying from alcohol poisoning and drug overdoses on prom night.

5. Consider taking someone in recovery as your date.

6. Focus on the dance, not on what is happening outside the dance.

7. Practice feeling sorry for your friends who are still caught up in and focused on drinking and drugging. It will only get worse.

8. Have that attitude of gratitude that YOU are clean and sober and can enjoy and remember this special event—your prom!

Prom Contract for Those in Recovery

Agreements	My Responsibilities	Consequences for Breaking Agreements
Teen: Remain clean and sober before, during, and after the prom.	Teen: Develop a recovery plan for the prom. Write it down. Ask for help or feedback for your plan. Show it to your guardian(s).	Teen: Without a plan for not joining many of your high school pals in their drinking/drugging behaviors, you are more likely to relapse.
Teen: Discuss with a sobriety mentor your date options. Be open to feedback.	Teen: Select a date who will be respectful of your recovery needs. Ask that person how he/she feels about no drinking/using on the night of the prom.	Teen: With a drinking/using or drunk/high date, it will be more difficult to honor your recovery by not joining in.
Guardian(s): Ask your teen what you can do to be supportive. If it is a legitimate request, do it. Teen: While you may feel you don't have the best relationship with your guardian, in this instance, tell them your prom plans, take in their feedback, and ask for help if you need it.	Guardian(s): It is not acceptable for your teen to shut you out of his/her prom plans. Find out what the schedule is. Do your research. Teen: There is to be no secrecy around your prom plans. Your recovery is critical to your health and future. Tell your guardian what you are going to do and how you plan to protect your sobriety.	Guardian(s): Drug and alcohol addiction only gets worse and worse. If you don't hold the prom requirements you have created, your teen will know that you have a tendency to not expend the energy it requires to help them guard their recovery. This opens a door for future contract violations and relapses. Teen: If you decide that you won't inform your guardian of your prom plans, you will forgo the event and attend a recovery meeting with your guardian instead.
Guardian(s): Become involved with the prom. Chaperone, cook, serve, or drive. Be the photographer. Be present.	Guardian(s): Share your teen's enthusiasm about the prom. If your teen is like many and appears very blasé, create your own enthusiasm.	Guardian(s): Lack of enthusiasm and participation will leave your teen to steer his own course through the prom. This might put added stress on his/her recovery.
Guardian(s): Help your teen celebrate prom time in a clean and sober manner. After prom, have your own celebration (out to dinner, cooking a special meal) in honor of their passage into a new stage of life.	Guardian: The day after prom, plan a day-time event for your teen and his/her friends. Lunch and a swim, brunch at IHOP, ziplining—think outside the box. This will give your teen more impetus to stay clean and sober during the prom.	Guardian(s): Involvement in your teen's recovery can be very subtle. If you don't become more "kid" oriented, your teen could struggle with recovery and lose the battle.

The Discussion About the Future

What will your teen do when he/she graduates from high school? For the college bound, this discussion usually begins in junior year (or earlier). Students and their parents have to deliberate about what colleges are affordable and are of interest to them. Our juniors and seniors have to take the SAT or other entrance exams. The results of these tests are submitted to the teen's selected universities and colleges for admission consideration. Often teens have to endure the laborious task of writing an essay that is submitted along with one's application. College applications are usually long and arduous. Picture the stress: Your teen must keep up with current schoolwork, study for tests, write research papers, AND pay attention to their college future and the demands that come with it—all at the same time. Are we tired just thinking about this?

There is also the consideration of what to do if your teen is not admitted to the colleges they wanted to attend. What is the plan then?

It is often no less stressful for those parents who have teens who want to be out on their own and have a career. There are three issues that arise: 1. What is your high school graduate qualified to do? 2. What does he/she want to do? Will it need more training? 3. The unrealistic views our teens have about what income has to be earned to be able to live on one's own. If you thought that the college parents were facing a lot of stress to aid their teen in the testing and application process, think again about what YOU are faced with! The college parents and perspective students have guidelines to follow. Each university/college has a written application and entrance process. You, on the other hand, have no written guidelines. This predicament can feel very lonely for parents of high school graduates. Where does one turn for advice? Start these conversations sophomore year and keep them going through junior and senior year until your teen has a plan.

The last thing to think about is what will happen if your teen does not graduate from high school or quits. For many parents whose teens are struggling with academics due to learning disabilities, drugs/alcohol, lack of ambition, or behavioral challenges, are we signing up for having a future of supporting a teen who could be working? What are we to do?

These are the issues that must be addressed with our teens as they make their way through junior and senior year. For four years, it is your teen's JOB to attend high school. There are few acceptable excuses. It is the law. Be sure that you, as a parent, do not let yourself inadvertently collude with your teen's reasons for not wanting to get an education. "I don't like school" is not a reason. "I don't want to go" is not a reason. "I won't go" is not acceptable. "I hate school" is a feeling, not a reason to drop out.

The Discussion About the Future: College Bound Contract

Agreements	My Responsibilities	Consequences for Breaking Agreements
Teen: Junior year, have a conversation with your parents about going to college. Make a decision, because there is a lot of work involved with getting into a university and you and your parents need time to plan.	Teen: Discuss college experiences with family members and the parents/older siblings of your friends.	Teen: You won't have the information necessary to make a decision about going to college versus getting a job.
Teen: Junior year, research colleges. Discuss your research with your parents. Ask your parents to take you to visit some of the ones you like. Parent(s): Make visiting colleges a fun experience for your family. Assist your teen with college research.	Teen: Research the grade point average (GPA) required by the colleges that interest you. If your GPA is lower is required, investigate other colleges/universities. Parent(s): Plan the trips.	Teen: You might end up wasting money applying to colleges where you don't meet the requirements. Parent(s): If you don't do your own independent research, you might end up having your teen apply to colleges where the entrance requirements and your teen's GPA and SAT scores don't match.
Parent(s): Research the dates to take college entrance exams (SAT) and help your teen sign up. Provide transportation to and from the test. If you think it would be beneficial, there are prep classes and tutors to help your teen prepare for college entrance exams. Discuss if your teen thinks this would be helpful. Make the arrangements.	Parent(s): Your teen needs your help in getting through the maze of the process of going to college. You will be in charge of this because your teen will not know how to do it by him/herself. Teen: Prep classes for the SAT can be very helpful. Ask your parents about this. No matter how intelligent you are, an SAT prep class can help you significantly increase your SAT scores. Go to it.	Parent(s): Without parental help, your good student could miss a chance to attend college! Teen: Even if you think you don't want to attend college, you might want to try it to see if your inclination was correct. That way you will have had a college experience and can make an informed decision. Otherwise, you won't know.
Teen: Senior year: 1. It might benefit you to take the SAT again to increase your junior year score. 2. Note the due dates for college application submissions. Parent(s): Assist your teen in making arrangements for prep classes and their second SAT test.	Teen: Ask your school advisors if they think taking the SAT test your senior year would benefit you. Ask your parents to help you with scheduling and paying for the test. Parents: Your help is a reward. Work with your teen regarding scheduling the SAT.	If parents and teens don't work together for the college experience, resentments about lack of parental support could develop.
Teen: May apply to four colleges. Parent: Will proofread the entrance essays your teen writes and mail the applications.	Teen: If you get accepted, congratulations. If not, get yourself into a local community college and make plans to transfer into the college of your choice.	Parent: If your teen doesn't get accepted to college, any belittling remarks will be remembered for years and perhaps break a bond of love and trust between you.

The Discussion About the Future: Going to Work

Troy

Troy wanted to go to work after graduation from high school. He thought he could make enough money working at a local coffee shop. He was tired of school and liked to work in a somewhat social environment. He thought he would work daily 8-hour shifts. He had not actually done any research about his job choice. He figured that once he got the job, it would "just work out." (This is a prime example of how difficult it is for teens to look into the future and plan for it. Their brain just isn't developed enough to give forethought to much of anything.)

Troy interviewed for the job and was excited when the boss called him to welcome him as a staff member. They arranged a meeting to "go over the details" of the job. Troy discovered that he would be making $9.00 per hour (minimum wage in his state). He did some quick math in his head: $9/hour × 8 hours a day = $72 per day. Then Troy multiplied that by 7 days a week and that equaled $504 a week! Troy was getting excited! He then wanted to know what he would make per month, so he multiplied $504 × 4 weeks in a month and BINGO! Troy was ecstatic to discover that he would be making $2,016 a month! That was more money that he ever dreamed of making! He was so excited that he allowed his curiosity to go one step further. How much would he be making a year? Well, 12 × $2,016 = $24,192! Troy thought he had won the lottery. He considered what car he would buy, what vacations he would take with his pals.

But then his attention was diverted back to what his new boss was explaining. Troy could work 4-hour shifts, 5 days a week. Of course, taxes and social security would be deducted. Troy didn't have any idea of what that would cost. (His net income would, in fact, be around $8,000 a year.) He tuned out the rest of the conversation. His bubble had burst. He felt depressed. Troy accepted the job because "it was better than nothing." He thought maybe he could find a second job. He had plans to move out of his mother's house and rent an apartment with a friend of his. Now Troy was unsure if he could afford it.

Teens can be so vulnerable to these types of situations. They get blindsided because they don't do the research on job options, and they have no idea about paying taxes. For those of us caregivers who have a teen who wants to go to work after high school graduation, it is necessary for you have many discussions about job choices and plans for living expenses. Coach your teen about how to deliver a good job interview. If you don't know, explore the Internet *with* (not for) your teen. Look for available jobs on Craig's List or other media sites. Notice the salaries that are offered.

Providing the safety net of education about how to interview and get a job, how to estimate tax deductions, and how to look for medical benefits will prepare your high school graduate for a more satisfying transition from high school to work. We can't teach ourselves what we don't know. Your teen will be set up to possibly make poor career choices without you being a mentor for them in this area. (See Chapter 7: Teens and Young Adults Living at Home for further ideas.) What if we caregivers, parents, guardians also have no idea about how to help your teen get educated about work after high school? Do the research together and make it fun. It is quite comforting for teens to learn their caregivers don't know everything.

The Discussion About the Future: Going to Work Contract

Agreements	My Responsibilities	Consequences for Breaking Agreements
Teen: Has decided to find a job after high school graduation.	Teen: Engage in conversations with your parents about how to find a job, what you think you would like to do, and how you propose to support yourself.	Parent(s): Without information, your teen will not be able to make educated decisions.
Parent(s): Discuss with your teen: 1. Job options 2. Pay and deductions 3. Ideas about living accommodations. 4. Preparing a resume. 5. Health insurance. 6. How to find a job. 7. Living expenses. 8. Part-time college—is your teen interested in that? (See Chapter 9: Going to College.)	Parent(s): Begin talking about jobs versus college during your teen's junior year. Help them learn about careers after high school by searching the Internet *with* (not for) them.	Parent(s): Being negligent about having these discussions will increase your teen's risk of failure. Nagging for the outcome YOU wanted will only serve to drive your teen away from the option you hoped they selected.
Teen: Research minimum wage in your state. www.ncsl.org/research/labor-and-employment/state-minimum-wage-chart.aspx is a great site with all-inclusive information.	Teen: Figure out if the job you are considering will allow you to earn enough to cover your expenses. Ask your parents about taxes that are going to be withheld from your income.	Teen: You might take a job that doesn't pay you enough. Yes, you can always quit and look for another job, but this takes so much energy. You could have done the up-front preparation and had a better outcome.
Teen: Where are you going to live? Discuss this with your parents.	Teen: Research the price of rentals in your area. Can you afford to rent an apartment or a room? Is it an option to continue living with your parents? Do you want to? For how long?	Teen: Living with no goals will keep you feeling like you are in high school.
Teen: How will I get to and from work? Have I figured that in to my living expense budget?	Teen: Review the schedules of public transportation. If you have a car, who is going to pay for gas and repairs?	Teen: It is important for you to have a discussion with your parents about this topic. Otherwise, you could take a job and have no way to get there!

The Discussion About the Future: Not Graduating From High School

If we caregivers have been on top of things, we will have a good idea about whether our teen is going to graduate from high school or not. Sometimes failure in high school is due to lack of parental involvement and attention. Sometimes parents try to guide their teens to make the most beneficial choices and they are met with opposition and out-of-control defiant behavior.

I have met those parents who are too occupied with their own careers, family issues, financial challenges, or addictions to spend time creating and enforcing school guidelines for their teen. According to these teens, the "lecture" for poor grades or not passing classes comes at report card time. The script goes like this: "You'd better pull yourself together and get through school" or "You can't go out with your friends, anymore" (more often than not, this fails to be enforced). It is much easier to "give the lecture" than to deal with the behavior that is keeping our offspring from passing high school classes.

I have also encountered many parents who have done "everything we can think of" to assist their teen with high school academic and social success. These parents come to my office in tears wanting to explore what they did wrong. They have provided tutors, been active in school activities, tried to interact with their teen by providing kind guidance. I have discovered that, sometimes, these families are too lenient in enforcing consequences, or one parent is more "forgiving" of abhorrent behavior than the other parent. Teens are so smart these days. They know how to divide and conquer: Pit the "soft" parent against the one who wants to enforce consequences for academic failures at school. This usually leads to arguments between the adults, and the teen does what he/she wants.

The issue is—whether you have been a disengaged guardian or a hands-on caregiver—if your teen doesn't graduate from high school due to academic failure, we all have the same problem: "*Now* what do we do?"

Some Things to Consider

1. How many years do you want your non-high school graduate to live at home?
2. What are the consequences for not graduating from high school?
3. Are you, the parents, willing to actively enforce your rules?
4. What about a GED (General Equivalency Diploma)? How would my teen get one?
5. I don't want my teen living on the street, but they are awful to live with. What are my choices?

For you or your teen to have a direction, the contract you create must address these questions. I can't tell you how many of my past patients have had their 35-year-old non-high school graduate still living at home playing video games all day. These parents are told that there are no jobs to be had. "I'm trying to get a job!" That's the standard response when these adults are asked, "What are you doing all day?" Then the 35-year-old "child" gets angry at her parents for being intrusive, and the parents tiptoe away because they hate conflict. Unless you want this fate, YOU are the one who must do the changing.

Contract: Not Graduating From High School

Agreements	My Responsibilities	Consequences for Breaking Agreements
You did not earn your high school diploma. We want to help you have a successful life. <u>Teen</u>: Sign up for the GED prep classes, attend them with no absences. Take the GED test. Pass the test. To research the GED a good site is AdultEd.about.com/od/glossary/g/GED.htm <u>Guardian</u>: Will pay for the GED classes and testing one time.	<u>Teen</u>: To research on the Internet about the location of GED prep classes near you. Find out the cost of the classes. Present the information to your guardian for review by June 10 of the year your class is graduating from high school. <u>Guardian</u>: Review the location and cost of the GED classes. Discuss how transportation will be provided. Arrange for who will be paying for transportation. Research free GED prep classes.	<u>Teen</u>: If you don't get your GED, you will be reduced to very low-paying jobs. The future will be difficult. <u>Guardian</u>: If you don't help your teen earn a GED, you will live with the fact that you didn't do everything you could to help him have a better career future.
<u>Teen</u>: You may live at home during the time you are taking your GED classes and test. No drug or alcohol use. Take drug test on demand. With one dirty drug test you will have to move out within 30 days. Be home by 11:00 P.M. on weekdays and 1:00 A.M. on weekends. A maximum of two hours/day on video games.	<u>Teen</u>: Attend your GED classes. Pass the test. No drugs/alcohol. Drug test on demand. Comply with curfew. Two hours/day on video games.	<u>Teen</u>: If you decide to violate these agreements, you will be given a 30-day notice to move out of the house and find other living accommodations. You may only take your personal belongings. If you do not pack yourself, on day 30 you will find your belongings boxed and at the front door for you to pick up. The locks will be changed to the house. <u>Guardian</u>: Being lenient on any one of these agreements will negate the contract. You will have created a credibility problem with your teen. This will lead to disrespect. (See Appendix A: Sample 30-Day Notice to Quit.)
Your guardian thinks that not graduating from high school is a serious issue and thinks that this lack of academic success is because you decided to not put forth the effort to conform to school and study guidelines. There will be strict adherence to this contract. For example, curfew at 11:00 does NOT mean 11:01. 11:01 is a violation of this contract.	<u>Teen</u>: This contract has no flexibility. Don't try to bend the rules. <u>Guardian</u>: Do not give any flexibility to the contract.	<u>Teen</u>: Any attempt to argue with your guardian about these guidelines will be considered a violation of this contract. You will be given a 30-day notice. <u>Guardian</u>: If you disregard the need for strict adherence to this contract, you are inviting your teen to negotiate the contract terms and to argue with you.
<u>Guardian</u>: Will not argue with teen about the fairness of this contract. <u>Teen</u>: How you feel about this contract is not the concern of your guardian.	**Arguing** <u>Guardian</u>: Tempting as it may be, do not engage in explaining or justifying this contract.	<u>Teen</u>: If you decide to create conflict about this contract, it will become null and void and you will be given a 30-day notice.
<u>Teen</u>: Sign a Release of Information (ROI) form so your guardian can have access to your school attendance records. This is to be done within the first week of school and a copy given to your guardian.	<u>Teen</u>: Sign an ROI at registration for the GED classes and give your guardian a copy.	<u>Teen</u>: If you don't sign the necessary papers that allow your guardian to see your school attendance and GED test results, your guardian will withdraw you from the classes and get a refund. You will be given a 30-day notice.

The Discussion About the Future: Quitting School

Caleb

Caleb was in 10th grade. He lived with his mother and his seven siblings. Caleb was the youngest, and all his siblings had completed high school and had jobs or were putting themselves through college. Caleb felt alone and unimportant. He felt ignored. He had struggled through 9th grade. School was challenging; he didn't understand math and he hated to write papers. In 10th grade, he longed to have friends to hang around with. At the beginning of the school year, Caleb met a guy who seemed to know everybody at school. Caleb thought of him as the "dude to know." He was shocked when this guy, Jerry, took an interest in him and wanted to hang out.

Caleb was invited to join Jerry and some of his pals in an area in back of the football field after school. As he approached the area, Caleb began to feel a little apprehensive. What was going to happen? Then he spotted Jerry with a group of pals, all laughing and having a good time. Jerry invited Caleb to smoke a cigarette and Caleb accepted because he had been smoking since 9th grade. Jerry gave him a "handmade" cigarette that Caleb instantly identified as a joint. Caleb and all of Jerry's pals smoked together and Caleb thought he had never had so much fun. He thought to himself, "I LOVE getting high and hanging with these dudes!"

Over the next few months, Caleb focused on his new friends and smoking and eating marijuana "edibles." He lost motivation to do much of anything else besides hanging out and laughing with his pals. In fact, Caleb was having so much fun he decided he didn't want to go to school. He quit.

Caleb began stealing from his mother and his brothers and sisters so he could support his daily pot habit and hang around with his pals. He learned that Jerry was the school drug dealer, who supplied a lot of students with various addictive substances. Caleb noticed that Jerry made a lot of money, and asked him if he would let him help sell drugs/alcohol as one of Jerry's "employees." He was ecstatic when Jerry agreed. The more Caleb sold to "customers," the more he would make. After a while, Caleb found himself "swimming in money"! He just knew he had made the right decision to quit school.

At the end of Caleb's 10th grade school year, his mother, Dorothy, found out that he hadn't been attending school. She discovered that Caleb's school had sent her a notification about his truancy, but Caleb had stolen it from the mail. She also learned that Caleb's school had sent automated phone calls, but Caleb had erased the voicemails before his mother returned home from work. She was furious. She scheduled a family meeting and enlisted her other children to try to talk sense into Caleb. Caleb became defensive and angrily left. Dorothy didn't know what to do. She was involved with a divorce, a stressful job, and felt overwhelmed by her own issues. She made an appointment with the school counselor. Together, they had a discussion with the school truancy officer about possible options to MAKE Caleb attend school.

Check your state for what the compulsory school attendance ages are. The following site offers helpful information: www.infoplease.com/ipa/A0112617.html. Caleb lived in a state in which the compulsory age for school attendance ended at 16. Caleb was going to turn 16 on August 1. There was nothing Caleb's mother could do about his quitting school. She felt guilty and devastated. Caleb blamed her for not giving him attention and having "time to date but no time for me."

Caleb's mother was a strong woman. While she didn't know quite what to do, she knew that there was a reason that her son had quit school. She had attributed his behavior changes to teen angst, but rethinking it, she realized that her son had undergone a personality change. She also recognized that Caleb no longer asked her for money. Because she wanted to save her son from bad decisions, Dorothy became a sleuth.

Eventually, she discovered that Caleb had gone into the drug dealing "business." Through inquiries with Caleb's old junior high school friends, Dorothy learned that Caleb had befriended Jerry, who was well known as the school's drug supplier. She felt heartsick. Caleb was still living with her, and she was afraid that he would have legal consequences for his work with Jerry. She was afraid that she would be held responsible for any drugs found at her house if it every came to a police search. Dorothy sought help from the Legal Aid Society and procured advice from a pro bono (free) attorney. She felt she needed some support and someone to talk to, so she contacted a therapist.

The following contract is how Dorothy dealt with Caleb's situation. Because his mother did not rescue him from his legal consequences for selling drugs, Caleb learned that he didn't want to spend his time incarcerated. He had repeated visits to juvenile hall. He hated his time there. Eventually Caleb procured his GED, and he now is in a recovery program and attending a vocational school to learn how to become an auto mechanic. If Dorothy had hired an attorney to reduce the legal consequences, Caleb would probably have continued on his course as a drug dealer. Dorothy views this contract as "Saving Caleb's life."

The Discussion About the Future: Quitting School Contract

Agreements	My Responsibilities	Consequences for Breaking Agreements
I, your mom, am saddened about you dropping out of school. I am also very unsupportive of your decision to sell drugs (fill in YOUR disappointment). Parent: I am giving you a 30-day notice to move out. I will not be held responsible in any way for your drug business.	Teen: Pack your things. Find a place to live. Turn in your house key. Remove all drug paraphernalia from this house. Parent: See Appendix A: Sample 30-Day Notice to Quit. Have someone witness your delivery of it.	Teen: If you do not pack your things, parent will do it for you and you will have to make arrangements to pick them up. Parent: You will have a drug dealing business being run from your home.
Parent: If you return to school before your 18th birthday, you may move back home if you are no longer selling or using drugs. Teen: Make arrangements with your school to find out what you will have to do to return.	**Return to School** Teen: Attend school. Be on time. Stay the entire day. Do your homework and turn it in. Parent: Have the school send you your teen's daily attendance/tardy record. Arrange to have weekly reports from your teen's teachers.	Teen: You will have to move out of the house. There is no second chance. Parent: You will not know if your teen is complying with this contract.
Parent: I will not hire anyone to represent you in court. Teen: If you are charged with violating the law, you will be on your own.	**Rescuing** Parent: Help your teen learn that living with the consequences of poor choices is worse than those associated with following the law. Teen: To manage any court proceedings in which you are involved. You will be in charge of getting your own public defender.	Parent: If you rescue your teen from consequences of his poor choices, you are teaching your teen that there really are NO consequences because he will be rescued by you. Teen: With no legal training in the area of defense, how do you think you will do in court?
Teen: 1. Will take a drug test on demand. 2. Will break connections with using/ dealing friends. 3. Will erase from cell phone the numbers of all drug selling/using connections. Will do this in parent's presence.	**No Drugs/Alcohol** Teen: Stop using drugs/alcohol while living at home. Disengage with using/selling friends and make an effort to find other interests. Parent: Will administer drug/alcohol tests on a regular basis and also arrange for teen to have viewed testing at a local lab.	Teen: You will have to move out of the house if you associate with drug activity in any way. Parent: If you decide not to implement this contract to the letter, you are giving your teen a good reason not to believe what you say and to disregard any part of this contract.
Teen: To be in a drug/alcohol treatment program starting when you move back home. Program to be at least two months. If you relapse, you will move out of the house. Sign a Release of Information so parent can see attendance and drug test results. Parent: Research affordable treatment options.	**Treatment** Teen: Comply with treatment expectations. Attend all sessions, be on time and stay the entire time. Parent: Check with counselors on a weekly basis to find out about attendance and drug test results.	Teen: Any relapse or unapproved absences from treatment will result in you moving out of the house. Relapse indicates that you are still in contact with dealers and/or using friends. Parent: If you don't follow through, you are enabling your teen to continue in the harmful activity of substance abuse.

High School Graduation!

Now that we have addressed the discussions about the future, let's focus on graduation!

"WOW!!! I'm an adult! Well, that's what the law says. But here's the secret! I don't feel like an adult, and I'm scared about what is going to happen next! But don't tell anyone. I'm expected to act grown up. The truth is, I don't know what I'm doing!" This is a quote from one of my past patients.

You know the future is really happening
when you start feeling scared!

While graduation is a huge life milestone and a rite of passage, it is often a very scary time of life! Some teens take graduation as a pathway to college. They know their life plan, and they picture themselves getting a degree and having an interesting career. But for many teens, this is a transition fraught with unknowns such as what it will be like to live away from the family. Are any jobs available? Can I take a year off and "just party"?

We parents have an opportunity to join with our graduating teens and make this a memorable time for them. We also have a chance to incorporate discussions about their future plans with graduation chatter. Flat-out ask your teen if he/she has any concerns about their life course after graduation. So graduation actually has two parts.

For the graduates:

1. Ditch Day—seniors leave the high school campus for a special outing
2. Finals
3. Did I pass? What if I didn't?
4. Graduation ceremony or no graduation ceremony
5. After-parties.

For the parents:

1. Notifying relatives
2. Planning a celebration for family and friends
3. A graduation gift.

At the beginning of senior year, go over the following contract.

High School Graduation Contract

Agreements	My Responsibilities	Consequences for Breaking Agreements
Ditch Day		
Teen: Have fun. Come home no more than an hour after the event. If there is drinking, no more than one beer. Or No alcohol/drug use. Comply with what your chaperones tell you to do. Parent(s): Research where the activity is taking place, who is chaperoning, what are the rules for attending the event? When does the event start and when is it over?	Teen: Inform your parent of the plans for and location of Ditch Day. Parent(s): Talk to one or more of the chaperones to discuss the Ditch Day plans. Give them your phone number in case your teen decides not to comply with the guidelines for this event? That way, you can pick them up. Who will pay for this event? Be clear with your teen.	Teen: If your parents don't have the necessary information by at least two days before Ditch Day, you may not attend. Parent(s): Lots of teens use poor judgment during Ditch Day. If you decide to not do the event research, you are leaving decision making up to your teen.
Finals		
Some teens know they will pass all their classes. For others, graduation can depend on passing a particular class. Parent(s): Be in contact with your teen's teachers regarding if they passed the necessary classes or not. Determine if they are graduating. If they are not graduating, cancel all graduation plans.	Teen: Study so you will pass the classes necessary for you to graduate. Ask your parent for a tutor if you need one. Be in reality—the grade fairy is not going to infuse you with enough knowledge for you to magically pass your finals. You have to earn your grades by studying. Parent: Early on in the junior/senior year, set up study guidelines and a homework schedule.	Teen: You will not graduate with your class. You will not attend the graduation event. Parent(s): See the Not Graduating From High School Contract, above. Your teen has not launched him/herself. You will benefit if you look at any part YOU had in this. Too lenient? Too busy? Too demanding? Too social? Too detached from your teen? Tired of being a parent?
Graduation Event		
Parent(s): Discuss graduation celebration ideas with your teen. Send out graduation announcements and invitations to the celebration. Find out how many guests you are allowed to invite to the graduation ceremony.	Teen: Discuss with your parent(s) what YOU would like to do to celebrate your graduation. Request a budget. Parent(s): Be open to your teen's ideas. While some parents might think a family gathering over a meal would be a great way to honor your graduate, your graduate might like to take a friend to a local theme park.	Parent(s): If YOU make all the plans without consulting your teen, whose event are you actually planning? Yours? Or your teen's? You have missed the chance to create your teen's, "most fun and memorable day," in honor of their accomplishment.
Family Celebration		
Parent(s): Consider if you can give your teen a special celebration day of his/her making AND a family celebration. Teen: If we don't like family get-togethers, sometimes we just need to please our family. Invite a friend!	Parent(s) and Teen: Discuss menu possibilities. Who? What? and Where?	This is a huge life accomplishment—graduating from high school. Parent(s): If you don't make a big deal about this, your teen will remember. Teen: If you are disengaged and disinterested in your graduation celebration, you don't get to blame your family for not being interested in honoring your accomplishment.
Graduation Gift		
Parent(s) and Teen: Discuss options and budget.	Teen: Once you know the budget, tell your parent what gift you would like for graduation.	Teen: If you don't voice what you would like, you might get something that you didn't want.

High School Graduation: You Never Graduate From Recovery!

Here is one more tribute to those high school students who are in recovery from drugs and alcohol. They have had a double job: They have had to pay attention to their studies and perhaps household chores or a job, as well as creating a life without drinking/using with their old buddies. There is no graduation from recovery. Once someone has an addiction, there is no future point at which one becomes a nonaddict.

I invite the caregivers of the teens in recovery to create graduation events where there is no use of alcohol, pot, or other drugs. I can't tell you the number of parents whose teens are in treatment around graduation time who say, "Well, we are serving wine at the family graduation dinner because the adults like it." I ask them, "Whose graduation party is this?" If your plans are NOT supportive of your teen's abstinence from all mind-altering substances, then change them. Do this because you are honoring three things: 1. Your teen's courage to be in recovery from substance dependence. 2. Your teen's accomplishment of graduating from high school. 3. YOUR commitment to do anything necessary to acknowledge and support your teen's sobriety.

Some parents say, "But I've asked my teen and he/she says, 'it's no big deal; it doesn't bother me.'" From years of experience with teens, I must share that the teens who report that their parents are having a "clean and sober graduation party" say this with such pride! They feel that their parents really understand their situation … that their parents went the extra mile and put the teen's needs first.

Clean and Sober Family Graduation Party

Brainstorm with your teen what he/she thinks would be fun.

Explore what your teen would like to serve to drink.

Have a conversation about meal choices.

Decide what games to play.

Where do you want to have it?

Maybe try something different.

Hire a fortune teller or some other entertainment.

Make it fun.

Gene, the fun fortune teller

CHAPTER 4

Love and Sex

Becky

BECKY: There was this guy named Paul. He was a senior. I had noticed him because everyone at school knows him. He's on the football team. I didn't think much about him until my friend Carolyn, who lives next door to him, told me he had been asking about me. I told her I thought he was cute and she told him. Then the next day at school he said, "Hi," and it sort of went from there.

THERAPIST: How did it go?

BECKY: Well, you know, he started talking to me, and then he asked me out, but I don't date yet, so we started kissing around the football field and holding hands, and then we became girlfriend and boyfriend.

THERAPIST: How long did that take?

BECKY: About two weeks.

THERAPIST: And then what happened?

BECKY: Well, we kinda snuck around. I snuck out of the house to be with him.

THERAPIST: What do you mean?

BECKY: Well… you know, since we were girlfriend and boyfriend we had sex.

THERAPIST: Why did you do that?

BECKY: DUHHHHH! We were girlfriend and boyfriend and I needed to prove that I loved him.

THERAPIST: Was having sex with him the only way to prove that?

BECKY: He said it was really important to him, and that I could prove my love for him, and we would get closer by having sex.

THERAPIST: Then what happened?

BECKY: We had sex for about a week and then he wouldn't talk to me or answer my text or phone calls. I'm bummed out. I can't eat. I don't care about school. I just want him back. We really loved each other, and now he is hanging around with some other chick. I'm so angry!

THERAPIST: Whom are you angry at?
BECKY: Him. (pensive) Me.

It took over a year to facilitate Becky in regaining her self-worth. It took just as long to help Becky discover what her values were regarding sex and love. She discovered that "proving" her love to a two-week acquaintance (or to anyone) by having sex wasn't actual love. It was infatuation. It was manipulation. It was NOT love.

Becky and I had lengthy conversations about how angry she was that her parents had not been informative about teenage love and sex. Becky reported that outside of the mechanics of menstruation and intercourse, she was left to explore that confusing area on her own. Her parents wouldn't let her date, so they thought she didn't need to know anything else. They wanted Becky to spend high school focused on her academics so she could get into a good college. They hadn't addressed the much needed emotional support that parents of teenagers need to give their offspring.

Becky's parents thought she was uninterested in having boyfriends. She had given them plenty of reasons to believe that their daughter could not have cared less about dating, much less a sexual encounter, because of all the disparaging remarks she had made about the guys at her school. One of the lessons we can learn from Becky and her family is that your teen can be one person at home and another at school. It becomes critical that we guardians of the next generation talk with our teens about dating, sex, teen love, and infatuation. We must guide them about how relationships can evolve and explain the difference between limerence (infatuated love that includes compulsive thoughts and fantasies) and actual love.

Becky's parents thought that "Becky is a really good kid and would never do anything to disappoint us. She wants to be in computer science, and we know she would never risk her goals by doing anything foolish." This was their belief before they noticed Becky becoming increasingly depressed and thus sought therapeutic help.

No matter what your teen is like, quiet and an A student or wild and caring less about school, we parents must educate ourselves about teen sex and teen love. We need to articulate our guidelines regarding high school romance, dating, steady boy/girlfriends and teen sex. We must come to terms with the fact that we guardians of teens are not going to stop our adolescents from having sex, but we can enlighten them with information about STDs, birth control, teenage pregnancy, etc. Educating your teenagers about this doesn't mean that you are promoting teen sex; it means you are educating them. Here are some statistics about teen sex from the U.S. Department of Health and Human Services: Talking with Teens:[9]

The likelihood of sex increases with each school grade level, from 32 percent in ninth grade to 62 percent in twelfth grade. Ten percent of all 13-year-olds have had sexual intercourse.

Adolescents who have sex early are less likely to use contraception, putting them at greater risk of pregnancy and STDs.

Many adolescents are engaging in oral sex prior to having sexual intercourse. About 51 percent of 15- to 24-year-olds had oral sex before they first had sexual intercourse.

_____

[9] _http://www.hhs.gov/ash/oah/resources-and-publications/info/parents/just-facts/adolescent-sex.html._

One in every five teenage girls will become pregnant during high school.

Half of all teenagers don't believe oral sex is sex.

Many adolescents are engaging in sexual behaviors other than vaginal intercourse. Nearly half have had oral sex, and just over one in ten have had anal sex.

Knowing the above information, just where do we parents begin our conversations about high school love and sex with our teens? What are our own values? What factors put teens at risk for making bad decisions? What family rules should be in place to guide our teens? It is not fair to our teens to have them enter high school without many conversations about behavioral and relationship guidelines. Consider the following:

Factors that Influence Adolescent High-Risk Behavior

From the National Longitudinal Study on Adolescent Health—Protecting Adolescents From Harm[10]

1. Involvement in violence
2. Emotional distress
3. Suicidality
4. Substance use
5. Parents being absent at waking, after school, at dinner and at bedtime
6. Lack of warmth, caring, and connectedness in the home
7. Lack of parent-and-adolescent activities
8. Adolescent working over 20 hours per week.

You will find that these topics are addressed throughout this book. High school love and sex has to do with teen health and emotional distress. What guidelines need to be created so our teens will be steered away from prematurely engaging in relationships that usually end in emotional turmoil?

---

[10] *JAMA,* The Journal of the American Medical Association, *September 10, 1997.*

From Dr. Phil McGraw[11]

1. Teenagers shouldn't have serious, romantic dating relationships. Adult supervised group dates should be encouraged.

2. Company that has a romantic potential should not be entertained in a bedroom. This rule should have no flexibility.

3. Parental guidelines and rules should not be too oppressive and restrictive. This only leads to rebellion. Discuss the rules with your teenager and work to co-create them.

4. Explain why you forbid certain activities. Your teenager will appreciate knowing that your guidelines are not arbitrary.

5. As a parent, it's your job to teach your teenager the importance of self-worth. Teenagers who value themselves as they are won't need to "find themselves" in other people.

6. Talk with your teenager. The more conversations you have, the less likely he/she will be to get into trouble. If you've always kept the door open for discussions, your child will be likely to come to you with questions or problems.

From **Better Homes and Gardens**[12]

1. Insist on a slow start. Do what you can to discourage early, frequent, and steady dating at least until age 16. Early, frequent, and steady dating is one of the single biggest risk factors for teenage sexual activity. Hold the line.

2. Establish dating rules and expectations. Establish rules early on for such things as curfews and dating activities—before your teen starts creating his or her own plans.

3. Teach your teen to date responsibly. Encourage your teenager to avoid sexually stimulating TV shows, videos, and movies when dating.

Teach your daughters to reject boys' lines, such as, "If you really love me, you'll do this for me" or "You know we both want to, so don't act like such a prude." And teach your sons not to say such things.

4. Don't allow your teens to date older persons. Teenage girls tend to have their first sexual experience with male partners who are three or more years older. For teenage boys, their first sexual encounter is likely to be with girls who are less than a year older. Be smart. Only allow your teenager to date persons of the same age.

5. Have them date in groups. Encourage your teenager to hang out in groups. When dating, encourage your teen to date with a buddy or friend. They can help each other out of difficult or tempting situations.

6. Always meet and greet. Insist that you meet the person dating your son or daughter each time before they go out. This will establish the message that you are watching.

---

[11] *http://www.drphil.com/advice/teens-and-dating.*
[12] *http://www.bhg.com/health-family/parenting-skills/teen-challenges/rules-for-teen-dating.*

From Dr. Laura Kastner, Associate Professor of Psychiatry and Behavioral Sciences at the University of Washington[13]

What does dating mean to teens now? What are the patterns and trends?

The term "dating" is hardly used anymore. Younger teens usually pursue their romantic interests via texts and third parties who scout out whether the other party is interested. Younger teens may "go out" (meaning: explore the idea of being a "couple") and break up and never even have a face-to-face conversation. Teens, especially those in high school and college, may refer to "hooking up," and that term can include anything from kissing at a party to sexual intercourse.

How can parents balance their need for information with their child's desire for privacy and independence?

It's all about mutual interests: Parents need information, and the teens need freedom. Parents should feel entitled to know what I call the Big 5: Where are you going? Whom are you going with? What is the transportation plan? Do you promise to call me if the plan changes? Do we agree on the curfew? If the teen blows it on following through, she or he has restricted freedom.

How should parents handle breakups?

Parents should offer empathy and compassion, and go light on the words of wisdom in an effort to make the teen less miserable. Comments like "There are more fish in the sea," or "You are young—you will have other loves in your life" are actually dismissive, not reassuring. A broken heart (remember Juliet was just shy of fourteen) can hurt as much, or more, than love at older ages. Be there for support, distraction and soothing.

From the Author

1. No matter when you start the conversations around family values regarding dating, teen sex, abusive relationships, teen pregnancy, some of what your teen does is out of your control. It is important to accept that.

2. Don't try to be your teen's "friend." So many mothers/fathers try to be part of their teen's social group. They think that this will provide closer bonding with their teen. When parents leave their own peer group to "be one of the girls/guys," they tend to violate their adolescent's privacy and inhibit discussions that are appropriate for teens. Guardians need to be there to provide well-thought-out structure, kind guidance, unconditional love, and consequences for violating the guidelines. We are there to be role models for what's OK and what's NOT OK.

3. Parents will find it valuable to have what I call "the high school discussion." This is a conversation with your teen about what your duties are as the parent of a high school student. Without such conversations, teens often can't figure out why their parents are "being so mean and strict."

---

[13] *https://mom.me/kids/teen/167-teen-dating-101.*

Your duties are:

1. To protect you from danger
2. Protect you from abusive relationships
3. To protect you from teen pregnancy and STDs
4. To protect you from putting yourself in risky situations
5. To support you in getting through emotional pain
6. To provide respect, love, and kindness as you transition through your teen years
7. To join you in celebrating your accomplishments
8. If indicated, to provide outside support for your struggles
9. To support and mentor you in reaching your goals

Discussion about each of these topics will assist your teen in knowing how dedicated you are to their high school safety and success. So many parents think they don't need to have these conversations because their "kids are good." You will bond more deeply with your teen through discussing your parenting plan with them.

4. Create a "(We Are Here to) Support You Through High School" contract. Put it in writing and give a copy to your teen. I have had so many teens tell me that it is comforting to read and re-read these contracts, "but I don't want my parents to know that."

Before you approach creating the "Support You Through High School" contract, be sure to review the statistics about teen sexual activity in Appendix B.

Support You Through High School Contract

Agreements	My Responsibilities	Consequences for Breaking Agreements
Parents: We are here to love and support you through high school. Our goal is to keep you out of harm's way while at the same time foster your independence. You may not like these guidelines. We will be the best parents we can be and these guidelines are created to help you have a successful life.	Parents: Live your values so you can provide your high school student with responsible role models. Respect this contract.	Parents: If you do not respect this contract, neither will your teen. The guidelines will become a topic for argument. YOU will NOT win.
Group dates beginning at age 16. No steady romantic relationships until graduation from high school. Date within your same age group. Teen: Introduce the people you group date with to your parents. Parents: Take an interest in your teen's pals and discuss with your teen what they like about each friend.	**Dating** Parents: Provide opportunities for your teen to entertain his/her social group at your home. Familiarize yourselves with your teen's friends and their parents. Teen: Be honest with your parents about where you are and whom you are with.	Parents: If you don't make the effort to know your teen's friends/acquaintances and their parents, you could be enabling your teen to put him/herself in high-risk situations. Teen: Not telling the truth about where you are and whom you are with will result in one of your relatives accompanying you to school for one week to meet your friends.
We support abstinence from sexual relationships while you are in high school. We acknowledge that if you decide you do not want to follow this guideline, we are somewhat powerless. Teen sex puts one at risk for pregnancy and STDs. Please advise us if you are having sex, and we will provide you with the necessary medical advice and protections. It only takes having sex one time to get pregnant or to get an STD.	**Sex** Parents: To discuss the risks of teen sex with your high school student. To accept that you are not able to control your teen's every behavior. Discuss teen sexual abstinence (see Appendix B). Discuss types of birth control. Inform your teen about STDs. Teen: While discussing sex with your parents can be embarrassing, your parents are a good source of information. Be curious. Ask questions.	Parents: Without this discussion, you could be leaving your teen to be guided by his/her peer group. That in itself is high risk. If you are judgmental or anxious about discussing sex and love with your teen, you will probably shut down future conversations. When that happens, a power and control struggle usually follows. YOU will not win. Teen: Without educating yourself about teen love and sex you put yourself at high risk for teen pregnancy, STDs, emotional pain, and a life of struggle.
Parents: We are here to help you avoid high-risk situations that could negatively affect your life. Abusive relationships, teen sex, meeting up with someone you don't know, sneaking out at night, or attending unsupervised parties are situations that lend themselves to high risk. We do not support you in participating in these activities.	**High-Risk Situations** Parents: Keep informed about whom your teen is socializing with. Do not waver from the consequences. Teen: Even though you may not think so, YOU are precious to your parent. Be honest about where you are going and whom you are going with. Know that part of a being a teen is to think that YOU are exempt from danger. In high-risk situations, this belief will not serve you well because YOU are NOT exempt from bad things happening to you.	Teen: *Abusive relationship*: attending groups at your local domestic violence center for one month. *Sex*: A visit to your pediatrician or Planned Parenthood. *Meeting up with a stranger*: Loss of cell phone and Internet for 30 days. For repeated infractions, cancelation of cell phone. *Sneaking out*: Bars on windows, alarm on your bedroom door, loss of cell phone for 30 days, and cancelation of teen's social media. *Unsupervised parties*: Your parents will come to the party and take you home, call police on the party, and contact the parents of the party host.
There will be no members of the opposite sex (for heterosexuals) or of the same sex (for gays and lesbians) or of anyone you are attracted to (for bisexuals and transgenders) allowed in any bedroom in our house unless a parent is with you.	**Guests** Parents: Have a responsible adult at home when your teen comes home from school, or pay a stay-at-home mom to watch your teen after school until you return from work.	Parents: Your teen will be on his/her own which invites high-risk situations. If you decide to leave your teen unattended, the responsibility for his/her bad decisions is mostly yours.

Sexual Orientation Issues

This section is not meant to be a discourse on different aspects of teenage sexual orientation. It is meant to give caregivers some information about the challenges and the risks faced by gay, lesbian, bisexual, and transgender teens. It is intended to provide us guardians of sexual minority adolescents with a path that would provide support instead of stunned judgment when our teens seem to be struggling with their sexual orientation. Many guardians of adolescents suspect that their teen might not be a heterosexual. They have no idea how, or if, they should begin a conversation. For other caregivers, they stand firm in the posture that "my teen is just misled," "it is a phase," and "being gay, lesbian, bisexual, or transgender is a mental health problem and requires psychiatric care." The adult confusion about how to address sexual orientation issues is mirrored by many teens. Neither group seems to know how to talk about it or how to proceed. But we have to break through this befuddlement and find a way!

I recently read an article about the heterosexual families of two 17-year-old boys. Each boy had gone to his parents and told them he was gay. One family told their son that he was loved and his sexual orientation was of no consequence to them. This son is living a happy life. He took a male date to his high school prom. He had support from his peers. The other family told their son that "it was just a passing phase," and got him counseling. They worked to counter what seemed natural to their teen. That son committed suicide. Sexual orientation issues are serious. They usually come up in high school. But please note that sexual orientation issues are not age specific. Often the struggle with sexual orientation begins way before puberty. Sometimes the acceptance that one is not a heterosexual is repressed until adulthood. I'm sure each of us has heard of people who "come out" (the process of declaring a homosexual identity) much later in life.

Before we discuss teen issues, let's have some vocabulary with which to discuss this topic:

Sexual orientation refers to whether a person's physical and emotional arousal is to people of the same or opposite sex. One does not have to be sexually active to have a sexual orientation.

Sexual preference has often been used to describe sexual orientation. Preference is an option; orientation is an act of nature.

Heterosexuals are attracted to the opposite sex.

Gays/lesbians are attracted to the same sex.

Bisexuals are attracted to the opposite *and* the same sex.

Transvestites get pleasure from dressing in clothing of the opposite sex. They may or may not be gay.

Transgenders' gender identity does not match their anatomy.

Homophobia refers to an individual's antigay attitude and behaviors.

Sexual prejudice refers to negative attitudes based on sexual orientation.

The Struggle

For sexual minority adolescents (SMA), life may or may not be a struggle. Most teens have challenges, and we should not ever attribute teen problems to being LGBT if there is no evidence or if it is not relevant. However, we must be sensitive to the fact that that many sexual minority adolescents face issues that are not generally present for heterosexual teens.

Lesbian, gay, bisexual, and transsexual (LGBT) youth are not a homogeneous group. For those who do struggle, the lack of congruity among them makes it difficult to concisely describe the inner and external conflict. Each is individual. The following highlights some of the components that can create struggle within sexual minority adolescents:

1. Challenges maintaining emotional stability and coping with internal and external stress due to low self-esteem

2. Fear of negative parental reactions to the disclosure of a sexual minority identity

3. Fear of family rejection

4. Being stigmatized within their schools or communities

5. Experiencing discrimination

6. Being bullied

7. Feeling isolated

8. Feeling ashamed

9. Fear of people discovering they are different

10. Despair that they will never be accepted or understood

11. Grief at not being like "everybody else"

12. Socioeconomic status, geographical location, culture, and religious beliefs also influence the intensity of the inner conflict of a SMA

As if the above possible fears weren't enough to deal with, they are often compounded by homophobic attitudes and social prejudice. As a result, risk for major depression, generalized anxiety disorder, conduct disorder, nicotine dependence, substance abuse and/or dependence, suicidal ideation, and suicide attempts is increased in the sexual minority adolescent population. Isn't it interesting that cultural mores and real or perceived judgments of authority figures and peers about how people have sex often seed these fear and shame-based struggles that can ignite mental health issues? Isn't it fascinating that many of us actually care about HOW others have intimate relations?

All young people...regardless of sexual orientation or identity deserve a safe and supportive environment in which to achieve their full potential.

HARVEY MILK

The following description of the "inner struggle" is a compilation of patient reports. Just the idea that these reports were from those who were having such significant issues with their sexual orientation that they sought counseling suggests that the depiction may be extreme and different from the norm. I offer it so we can have some idea, extreme or not, of how the identity struggle develops and evolves. We also might benefit from noting some of the following has also been reported by teens with weight, physical, social, and academic challenges.

The Inner Conflict

From elementary school on (and sometimes before that), children learn insecurities. As they enter school, parents lose their dominant importance, and a child's greatest influences become people in their neighborhood and their school. School-age children learn to take on attitudes of the surrounding world. They internalize stigmas. As they mature through middle school and high school, they develop a sense of personal identity and a direction for the future. Sexual minorities gradually become aware of same-sex attractions, and of the mainstream bias against homosexuality. They may experience gender confusion.

Through each stage of development, kids compare themselves to others; do they see themselves as being similar to or dissimilar from their peers? While most children, preteens, and adolescents pass through stages of feeling "awkward," many sexual minority children have reported that, inside, they feel they don't fit in anywhere. They see themselves as "dissimilar," but so often that they can't identify just why they feel that way.

In an effort to disguise their feelings of undefined "dissimilarity" from family and schoolmates, some act out, others isolate. Some become the class and family comedian. Some make a lot of friends. Others become loners. Some focus on excelling in sports or academics, while others pursue more artistic interests like drama and music. Whether they deal with their feelings of "dissimilarity" through joining or disengaging, inside they still feel alone. The mirroring by schoolmates serves to underscore that their peers also perceive them as "different." The belief for most school-age sexual minorities is that if one's peers see you as dissimilar, then it must be true. You ARE alone! Until one can identify just why they feel different, the inner turmoil can feel like chronic anxiety and/or depression.

Hiding any type of divergence from school peers is usually a battle that is not won because kids seem to have a sixth sense about who is "apart." Once dissimilarity is noted, there is a dynamic that is created: The "dissimilar one" is the recipient of the most hurtful things their peers can think to say to them. These "dissimilar" children begin to feel like there is no safe peer with whom to authentically interact and this feeds the formation of the social mask and the search for connection and engagement with almost anyone who is nice to them.

The dynamic of "if you're nice to me I'll be your friend" is a common one throughout grammar and high school. As noted above, it is during these school years that adolescents learn their personal identity and discover a direction for the future. They learn how to select friends and they hang out with people who have interests in common. However, if one's main personal identity becomes "dissimilarity" and if the goal for one's future becomes "belonging," it is the striving for acceptance that evolves into the driving force of one's life. This can cause problems because "belonging" is often sought without restraint and without a screen for potential danger, abuse, and violence.

A patient of mine recounted how this dynamic took control of his relationships:

I have spent my life trying to be like everyone else. I did everything I could do to fit in, but I never discovered how. I knew I was different, even if I didn't know why. The kids at school saw me as different but, like me, they didn't define why they saw me that way. I became a star on the swim team and a good student. I had friends—but I didn't let them really know me. Over time, I became aware that I was attracted to guys, not girls. I felt fear and shame. I tried to hide it, even from myself. I wanted to be like everyone else. I felt confused and like I didn't belong anywhere.

I dated girls. I wanted my feelings of attraction to guys to be a passing phase. So I sought out female companionship. I wanted to have the experience of being in a heterosexual relationship. I tried to fall in love with the first girl who paid attention to me, but sex with her was repugnant and she was a pothead and was always stoned. I isolated.

In college I found someone I could relate to. For the first time in my life, I met a guy who was really interested in ME; he was nice to me, and I immediately got into a sexual relationship with him. He took me to LGBT groups. He understood me. I was in love. I thought I had found that place of "belonging." Then he beat me and became so verbally abusive I contemplated suicide. This cycle has repeated over and over in my life. Why can't I find someone who is safe? Someone who is nice?

Most sexual minority adolescents experience pieces of this patient's process with accepting his sexual orientation. Let's review:

1. A feeling of being "different." Trying to overcome "dissimilarity"
2. Realizing that the difference relates to sexuality
3. Comparing one's identity to others
4. Disclaiming one's internal truth and trying to pass as straight
5. Acceptance of one's sexual orientation
6. Learning how to be LGBTQ. (This is often very challenging.)

For a rewarding and normalizing conclusion to the process of accepting one's sexual orientation, many SMAs divide the world into "straight" and LGBT. As they mature, they develop pride in their subculture, and work to integrate it into their community. They learn that their sexual orientation is only one part of their identity.

However, if there is no recognition of or support for the internal struggle that accompanies the process of acceptance of one's sexual orientation, SMAs may become stuck in the paradoxical world of passive surrender that their life was meant to be a struggle and there is no peace:

1. I want to be "similar," but I'm "dissimilar."
2. I want to belong, but I don't belong anywhere.
3. People who are initially nice are usually mean.
4. I want to be heterosexual. I think I'm gay (lesbian, bisexual or transsexual, or unsure). I am confused.
5. When I compare myself with others, I feel alienated. I want acceptance.
6. I am sad. I want to be happy.
7. So I came out, which was supposed to be freeing. I am still "dissimilar," because I now have to identify as gay (lesbian, bisexual, transgender, or unsure).

What is your reaction to the above-described struggle that is all based on how people have sex? Perhaps as we begin the escorting of our adolescents to adulthood, we would benefit from some introspection about our own biases, the way we interact with those who are different from the mainstream, and the phenomena of cultural disempowerment based on sexual orientation. The struggle of the sexual minority adolescent is not linear. If one becomes stuck in the contradictions between the heterosexual and the sexual minority world, strife will prevail. The difficult thing for us guardians is that if our teens are struggling with their sexual orientation, there is no way we can eliminate the internal conflict for them. As previously noted, some struggle more than others. How can we be supportive?

1. Educate yourself.
2. Check your own bias. Get counseling.
3. Realize that your teen's sexual orientation is NOT about YOU. Maybe YOUR dreams for biological grandparenthood, or the white-lace bridal dress on your son's bride are not in your future.
4. Be a safe person for open sharing.
5. If your son/daughter comes out to you, do NOT say, "Oh honey, it doesn't matter! We love you no matter what!" How that sentence is often interpreted is, "Even though there is something wrong with you, we love you anyway." A better response is, "We respect the person you are."
6. Give your SMA the freedom to find his/her own way. If they seem lost, counseling with an experienced professional may be helpful.
7. Many parents do all sorts of research on sexual minority teens. Good for you if you are one of them. However, from that information, please don't make a menu of possible things your teen could join to "help" them. Often parents suggest to their SMA that they join the high school LGBT group. Some, but not all, teens have reported that this suggestion serves to verify their "individuality."
8. As guardians, we all have the responsibility to keep our teens safe. Members of the LGBT community are at higher risk for victimization. Be aware.
9. No matter what a teen's sexual orientation is, the dating, curfew, and safety contract agreements are the same. This includes the pregnancy component because adolescents have been known to experiment.

There should be no discrimination between siblings based on sexual orientation.

We all would benefit from stepping back and realizing that many of our sexual minority adolescents are so resilient that they often turn out to be the creative innovators of our society. For us caregivers, work to be understanding. Strive to be accepting. Endeavor to interact with your SMAs just like you do with anyone else—after all, they *are* "anyone else," unless we make it so they aren't.

CHAPTER 5

Sibling Rivalry and Abuse

Tiffany

Every day when she returned from work, Carolyn would be greeted by her tearful 14-year-old daughter, Tiffany, crying that her two older (and much larger) brothers had hit her, taken one of her belongings, or were teasing her about her weight. Tiffany had made these reports so often that her mother considered them "normal." Carolyn reported, "Tiffany can be very whiny at times, and she teases her brothers. Her brothers blame Tiffany for starting disputes, and Tiffany blames her brothers for coming into her room and taunting her. They argue about who started it. I don't know whom to believe, so I send all of them to their rooms. I just don't know what to do, and I feel like a referee. I'm not effective because I'm not there to see what goes on."

Sibling abuse is often referred to as "fights," and many parents presume that conflict will happen between their children. And that is usually an accurate expectation. There are very few siblings that don't argue about one thing or another. Many parents also expect aggressive behavior between siblings, and these notions serve to normalize teasing, combative physical contact, and cruelty. If this is allowed in anyone's home, where is the safe place for a child to live? If not in the home, where? Tiffany described it as follows:

> My brothers teased me on the school grounds. They called me "Miss Piggy." All the other kids learned to call me that too. My life was miserable. Then I'd get home, and my brothers would gang up on me. Either Barry or Justin or both would come in and hit me for nothing. Or I'd be trying to do my homework and they'd shuffle my books and papers on the desk. I'd get mad because my papers would become all wrinkled.

> Then Mom would come home and they'd blame me for coming in their room and calling them a name and they'd tell her, "Tiffany started it!" I have no safe place to be because my brothers are always around making my life miserable. Even when I have friends over, they're all in our business, calling me names. I hate them.

Because of the interactions with her brothers, Tiffany really didn't have a safe place. Additionally, her mother didn't provide one because she viewed it as "typical sibling fighting," and since they all blamed each other, Carolyn didn't know who was at fault. Tiffany's father tended to "punish" her brothers by whipping them with belts, and because Carolyn couldn't bear to watch how he did this, she rarely reported to him about what went on at school or in their house after school. Tiffany had no one to protect her.

How do we define sibling abuse?

It is important to differentiate between sibling rivalry and sibling abuse. Rivalry is a commonplace occurrence between siblings. It is about calling each other mean names, and arguing. It is about contending for the attention and affection of caregivers. Sometimes it can lead to physical attacks. However, rivalry can manifest in healthy competition among siblings and lead them to learn interpersonal and social skills. Sibling abuse is the physical, sexual, or emotional abuse of one sibling by another wherein one child is always the victim and the other child is always the aggressor. It frequently mirrors the parent/parent and the parent/child relationships. Sibling abuse can cause long-term problems. Although it is often overlooked by guardians, sibling abuse is more common than parental or spousal abuse.

Birth Order

The Oldest Child

When a second child arrives into the family, the oldest one usually resents the attention that becomes redirected to the new arrival. The oldest child feels abandoned because the spotlight that used to be theirs is now on an infant.

a. The oldest child can get blamed for things the youngest child did.

b. The oldest sibling is given responsibilities at far earlier ages than their younger brothers/sisters.

c. The younger children are resented because their older sibling perceives them to have it much easier and with less scrutiny that is accompanied by preferential treatment.

d. Because the oldest child is bigger in size, he/she can use stature as a way to intimidate, boss, and dominate their younger siblings.

The Middle Child

Many middle children feel ignored and forgotten. They can view themselves as least favorite or as being an outsider.

a. They often perceive that their older sibling is more loved than they are.

b. In an effort to gain favor from their caregivers, middle children often try to demonstrate the ability to be responsible by caring for their younger siblings in a controlling manner.

c. Middle children can be rebellious.

d. Due to the lack of attention at home, middle children often have low self-esteem.

e. Avoiding conflict by being a peacekeeper can become a way of trying to please parents and friends. Consequently, the middle child can enter arguments without an invitation to do so. This can trigger resentment because this child is in everyone else's business. It can also lead to avoiding one's own problems because one is focused on the difficulties of others.

The Lastborn Child

As parents have more than one child, their focus on childrearing becomes somewhat lackadaisical. Let's face it: Parents get tired! Thus lastborn children often seek attention from their caregivers by being fun-loving, and outgoing. They learn to be congenial, and sometimes they use this trait to manipulate adults into overlooking irresponsibility.

a. Being the baby of the family, the youngest child is often treated preferentially and is sometimes indulged by parents and other relatives.

b. Older children can view the lastborn child as a spoiled brat.

c. The youngest child can be the "poison container" for their elder sibling's jealously and thus be the main recipient of routine emotional, verbal, and physical retaliatory treatment.

d. Humor, whining, asking for help, and joining with younger siblings against the eldest one are some ways lastborn children find their way through the sibling rivalry dynamic.

Favoritism

Siblings vie for parental favor and one child being best-liked fosters resentments. This can lead to less-favored children monitoring the behavior of the favorite sibling in order to prove to the parent that the favoritism shown their brothers/sisters is undeserved. If the rivalry dynamic of "I'm good" and "you're bad but people don't see you for what you are" becomes chronic, families often maladapt, and the parent's life becomes one of being a referee between siblings reporting the errors of each other.

The Unfavored Child

Unfavored children struggle for parental love because they feel like every family member is better than they are. The adults as well as the brothers and sisters in their life compare the unfavored child to others in the family, and the unfavored one usually comes up short. This dynamic can feed the desire to retaliate and seek revenge for being the "outcast." Often the unfavored child is the middle one. This is due to parental doting on the oldest, who usually experiences each life milestone first, and then to the parental adoration of the baby, who needs the help and nurturing afforded an infant. The middle child often is left out and thus views him/herself as "unfavored," ignored, underappreciated, and not valued as being an individual.

Unfavored children often have low self-worth. They may be different from their siblings. One's brothers might be into athletics while the unfavored male might prefer artistic endeavors. They may be out of sync with their parents. Extroverted caregivers could easily overlook an introverted, shy offspring. These factors can lead to sibling aggression, hostility, and verbal, emotional, and physical misconduct.

Competitive Environment

What would stimulate rivalry more than growing up in a competitive environment wherein siblings and parents strive for the "win" against each other? And just what is this "win" about? It is about earning the parental reward of attention and acknowledgment. It is about outdoing one's siblings so one can be favored—if only temporarily. A family dynamic that is based on competitiveness usually teaches siblings that one's self-worth depends on "winning." Do we give consideration to those who don't win that round of competition?

Competitiveness between family members can lead increased self-esteem and sophisticated social skills. It can also lead to feelings about never being sufficient unless there is a "win." For those who "won," often, a posture of entitlement can develop because, after all, that person proved himself/herself to be better than their siblings. What started out as healthy competition can evolve into a goal of besting one's brothers and sisters, no matter what the cost. Competitiveness for power in the family often leads to abuse.

When all the needs of individual personalities, family dynamics, and other external factors converge on a family, it is understandable how sibling abuse can develop. Each child's pull for love, attention, acknowledgment, and favor often becomes so overwhelming and chaotic that the family atmosphere can evolve into a bitter, undifferentiated and unbearable mass of extremes: The "winner" and the "loser," the "good kid" and the "bad kid," the "smart one" versus the "dumb one," the "geek" against the "party dude," the star athlete versus the one who hates sports, and so on. When the state of the family environment is such that children are not recognized for their individual talents and are pitted against each other for a stardom that mirrors their parents' (and maybe not their) interests, they cannot get their needs met. This becomes the ripe arena in which the seeds of sibling abuse are sown.

Risk Factors of Sibling Abuse

What are the risk factors that might create an environment that invites sibling abuse? According to the University of Michigan's Health System research,[14] the possibilities are numerous:

Absent parents
Emotionally distant or uninvolved parenting style
Acceptance of sibling rivalry and fights as, "normal," and therefore ignoring them
Little parental instruction about how to handle conflict in a healthy way
Fostering increased competition among siblings by planning favorites and comparing children
Allowing violence between siblings
Having the oldest sibling take care of the younger ones
Exposure to violence at home, in the media, in video games, neighborhood bullying
Not teaching one's children about sexuality and personal safety
Increased violence over time between siblings
Negative sibling interaction
Children having witnessed sexual abuse or having been victimized by it
Access to pornography

---

[14] *http://www.med.umich.edu/yourchild/topics/sibabuse.htm.*

Components of Abuse

How do we know it is abuse? Sometimes we think that sibling "horseplay" is the normal course that sibling interaction takes. I think it is important to view sibling abuse as another form of domestic violence. Does that sound extreme? There is so much new research that is now identifying sibling abuse as sibling assault, as a violent struggle for power, as an undeserved physical and emotional battering, as a relationship based on fear of one or more siblings, and as living in an environment in which the "punishment" by the sibling doesn't fit the "crime." It has been found that in many of the families in which sibling abuse takes place there is a paucity of guidelines that will assist kids in knowing the parameters of sibling interaction.

When Does It Become Abuse?

As we mentioned in the introduction to this section, sibling abuse occurs when one brother/sister emotionally, physically, or sexually inflicts harm on another sibling. Sibling abuse includes hitting, biting, kicking, beating, threats of mortal injury, and using weapons to inflict physical harm. It encompasses sexual behavior between siblings that is motivated by other than age-appropriate curiosity. Often one sibling blames the victim as being the cause of a violent interaction. With sibling abuse, discovering who started a disagreement just doesn't matter. What does matter is that we protect our offspring from what can turn out to be sibling abuse trauma.

In the last decade, sibling sexual abuse has come out from the closed doors that helped protect family secrets. When reported, there are laws in place that deliver consequences to the abuser. However, it is a topic that is still largely unaddressed. The reason for this is because the caregivers and the victims are the ones who have to do the reporting; the parents have to counter their protective instincts and the victim fears for his or her life. Often parents rationalize why sibling sexual abuse happened: "Johnny was experiencing normal teenage curiosity and it went too far" or "Suzie is just way too precocious." They try to salve the wounds of all parties involved without having the knowledge about how to handle sexual abuse. This serves to re-victimize the victim. At the same time, the victim is often questioned and re-questioned regarding the legitimacy of their report.

Although I am not in the legal field, as a psychologist I cannot think of many laws that specifically address nonsexual sibling abuse. Therefore, we caregivers of children and teens have to be the makers and enforcers of the rules. We can no longer ignore reports when our teens tell us they have been victimized by a sibling. We can no longer tell ourselves that one sibling "deserved" what their brother/sister did to them. Pretending the issues don't exist, blaming the victim, or believing the violent interactions will go away all serve to keep sibling abuse alive and well in one's family. If sibling abuse is not happening in your family it may still be beneficial to address it and to address how to resolve conflict. If we guardians did not start this process when our teens were little, or if our teens evolved into siblings that feed on arguing with each other, it is never too late to define what the parameters are attached to these interactions.

Parental Interventions

If sibling rivalry and abuse is taking over your family life, it is time to put a stop to it before one of your teens victimizes a sibling to a point that emotional, physical, or sexual violations become a normative aspect of their interactions. We must also be cognizant that sometimes the victim takes out their frustrations and emotional pain on their peers. How do we address these issues in our families?

- Learn about conflict resolution and anger management. Arrange for your teens to learn about these subjects from someone other than you.
- Get rid of ideas that foster sibling abuse such as: "Kids will be kids," "What happens at home is the family's business," "All brothers and sisters call each other names."
- Reduce the rivalries.
- Don't compare your teens.
- Eradicate the idea of "good" and "bad" siblings in which the bad one harasses the good one, who is perceived as the innocent victim.

- Intervene on your teen's intersibling conflicts to prevent escalation to abuse.
- Model nonviolence for your teens—this would include lack of support for sports team members who resort to physical violence to address differences.
- Create a contract addressing sibling abuse.
- Do not blame the victim.
- Have your words and actions mirror each other. It is contradictory to tell your teen not to hit her 5-year-old brother as she watches you spank him.
- Practice consistent and fair-minded parenting.
- Interact with each teen in an equal manner.

The following contract will assist us parents in intervening before rivalry becomes unhealthy and abusive. Sexual abuse is not included in this contract because reporting it to the proper authorities is the best way to protect the victim from the abuser. The consequence for sibling sexual abuse has to be protection of the victim from the perpetrator—no matter what!

The Arguing Cycle

Dear Caregivers of Teens,

If you get into a power struggle with your teens and find yourself arguing with them, you have taken their "debate hook," and YOU will lose! The arguing cycle usually begins with a teen not agreeing with some decision or guideline that their parent has made. This leads to the parent trying to explain, justify, or provide a rationale for why their teen isn't being allowed to do something, or why they lost a privilege. The unfounded expectation of most caregivers is that if their teen understands the reasons behind not being able to do something, the teen will have that "light bulb moment" and say, "Oh thank you for explaining that to me, I'll do it your way." I have *never* seen that happen!

When there is a rule or decision your teen disagrees with, there is no need to explain. Ask the question, why do you think this is a house rule? Or, why do you think we made this decision? The usual response from a teen who wants to argue their parent to "emotional fatigue" and surrender is, "I don't know; it's a stupid rule, and I'm not going to follow it." This is usually accompanied by some sort of departure from your presence and a slammed door. (What's the family guideline about slamming doors?)

The caregiver response to this is either to ignore it, or to immediately try to further explain. These explanations become repetitive, and eventually your teen will tune YOU out. YOU are the one who will be frustrated and tired. Often, teens can wear their parents out to the point that the parents give in to the teen's wants. When parents "give in," it is a "touchdown" for the teen! They now know the secret to exhausting you to the point that you "give in" and violate your own guidelines and your better judgment. One "give in" and YOU have rewarded and reinforced the arguing cycle.

Teen disagrees with parental decision/guideline →

Teen becomes angry and tries to argue his/her reason for not liking it or wanting to comply →

Parents try to explain the reasons behind their decision →

Teen gets frustrated and emotional and leaves their parent's, "conversation" →

Parents attempt to make peace and re-explain →

Teen tries to wear down their parent's resolve →

Outcome →

1. Teen wears the parent down so they give in to teen.
2. Parents try to repair the emotional argument by further explaining their position.
3. Consternation and antagonism fill your house.

Crystal

Crystal was 16 years old, on the debate team at her high school, and enjoyed practicing her skills on her single father, Henry. Everything was an argument/debate. Crystal became quite adept at twisting a phrase, producing unsubstantiated "facts" to support her position, and arguing to "win." Crystal's father thought that if his daughter understood his reason for saying "no," she would concede to his elder wisdom. Time after time, his belief was proven incorrect.

One Friday, Crystal advised her dad that she was going out with some friends. When asked who they were, Crystal replied, "You don't know them." The conversation continued as follows:

HENRY: You know the rule, Crystal: I have to have the names of the people you are going out with, talk to their parents, and you need to tell me where you are going.
CRYSTAL: I'm 16 now, Dad. That is the stupidest rule! I'm a good student, I excel at debate, and you don't trust me. Why should I bother to do anything you want?
HENRY: I just need to know that you are with good people and that you are safe, that's all.
CRYSTAL: No one else's parents make them provide all the shit that you want. And talking to their parents? That's just insulting! I have no freedom. How am I ever learn how to be independent? You are suffocating me! Mom would have never kept me in prison like you do. (A made-up conclusion, sounding like fact.)
HENRY: Well, I don't think it is too much to ask to know whom you are with and where you are going. I love you so much and, after all, you're the only thing I have now since your mother died. (Guilt.)
CRYSTAL: You just don't understand, and if I can't go, you will ruin my life, because this is the popular group and I have been working hard to get in it. Now I'm invited to be with them and you ruin my chances!
HENRY: Sweetie, all I'm trying to tell you is that I need to know the names of the kids you are going out with and I need to talk with their parents. I also want to know where you are going.
CRYSTAL: Well, I'm going out anyway, and you can't stop me. (Power play.)

Without a word, Henry went out to Crystal's car and disconnected her starter. He collected her cell phone and, as was noted in his contract, kept it for a week. Henry did some investigation through Crystal's friends that he did know. It turned out that the "popular kids" were having a party at a home where the parents were away on vacation. Henry later discovered that the police were called that night and the event made the front page of the newspaper in his town. A girl had been raped. Drugs were found on the premise. This event reaffirmed Henry's determination to respect the "Support You Through High School" contract he had gone over with Crystal. Yay for Henry!

Could Henry and Crystal's verbal interaction been shorter? Could it have been less argumentative? An old adage says, "You don't have to attend every argument you're invited to." Here's one way:

CRYSTAL: I'm going out tonight just to hang out with some of the popular kids.
HENRY: Do I know them?
CRYSTAL (defensive, heated): No Dad, you don't know them. I'm not a baby anymore. These are good kids. Your rules are stupid. I feel like a prisoner.
HENRY: Honey, this must be tough on you.
CRYSTAL: No shit, Dad! You are so nosey into everything I do, and I hate it. I have no privacy. You want to interrogate all my friends. You make me look like an asshole.
HENRY: So tell me what you wanted to do.
CRYSTAL: Well, we were just going to hang out!
HENRY: Where?
CRYSTAL: I don't know yet! They are going to let me know. Geeeeeze! (Becoming more guarded and defensive.)
HENRY: Well, when you find out, let me know, and we'll talk further.

This puts it all back on Crystal, who knows the guidelines of her father. She can't tell her father that there is a party at some home where the parents are on vacation. However, she could lie:

CRYSTAL: I found out it's at Mike's house and his parents are home.
HENRY: Do I know Mike?
CRYSTAL: He's just the quarterback on the football team.
HENRY: Well, get me his phone number, and I'll talk to his parents and we'll discuss it more after my conversation with them.

Of course, Crystal can't deliver. She gets upset and emotional. Notice there are no explanations, there are no arguments except the one Crystal is having with herself. She might have a temper tantrum, but it doesn't matter because her father kept her safe from a very high-risk situation.

Sibling Rivalry and Abuse Contract

Agreements	My Responsibilities	Consequences for Breaking Agreements
We members of this family need to love and support each other. These guidelines are intended to assist us in having a family in which we are kind and respectful.	Teen: Treat your brothers and sisters with respect even if they are mean and disrespectful to you. Do not participate in seeing who can be the meanest. Guardian: Intervene in your teen's arguments when they become demeaning or physical. Have a list of family "cleanup" projects at hand. Set aside times when you will be available to monitor each project. You might have to set aside an entire day and evening until your teens become cooperative with each other.	Teen: 30 minutes of participation in a family cleanup activity such as washing the car, weeding a section of the garden, etc. This will be monitored by a guardian and done during a time when they can watch. One 30-minute cleanup activity will be followed by another until siblings cooperate with each other in completing a task. Guardian: Lack of correction in this area can give tacit permission for emotional and physical sibling abuse.
Emotional abuse includes ridiculing, insulting, humiliating, or threatening your brother(s) or sister(s). Destruction of your sibling's personal property is also emotional abuse.	Teen: Learn that if you can't say something nice, don't say anything at all. Answer the question to yourself, "How do I feel about myself when I'm mean to my sibling?" Guardian: There is a nice way to teach your teens how to interact with each other and then there is a way in which your teens are left to their own, often abusive ways of sibling interaction. You are the role model and the teacher. Instruct your teens! Get instruction about conflict resolution for yourself.	Teen: Attend conflict resolution classes in order to learn how to resolve disputes in a healthy manner. Teen will participate in these until he/she becomes proficient in resolving sibling conflict. Guardian: We can't teach ourselves what we don't know. Teens need guidance. If you choose to ignore cruel sibling interactions you are covertly approving them. What we don't correct becomes "OK."
Physical abuse includes hitting, biting, kicking, threatening injury.	Teen: There is NO physical cruelty in our family: that includes poking, tapping, or tickling such that your sibling asks you to stop. Guardian: We must protect all our teens against physical abuse. While it may start out as play, it can evolve into cruelty. State the parameters clearly and enforce the consequences for violation of them.	Teen: Physical altercations between teen/any sibling, will testify to the need for anger management classes. These will be attended until your behavior indicates you have mastered how to control your anger. Sibling who was the recipient of physical abuse will be given self-defense classes of the type that doesn't inflict physical harm such as tai chi. Guardian: Allowing teen physical abuse can create a life of trauma for the victim.
Competition is normal between siblings. Winning at something is great! It doesn't mean we guardians love you more because you excelled. We love you equally and respect your individual talents.	Teen: Let your guardian know what your interests are: sports? art? drama? foreign language proficiency? If you don't know, try them all. Guardian: Be aware that your interests might differ from your teen's. Respect individuality. Help your teens to not compete against each other.	Teen: If competition between siblings in a particular area of interest leads to physical/emotional abuse, both parties will be separated from that interest, and supported to find activities separate from their sibling. For example: If being on the same football team spurs violence between the siblings, both shall resign from the team and pursue other interests. Guardian: If you don't end the competition that leads to abuse, it will continue.
Teasing occurs when we want to hurt someone else's feelings.	Teen: Do not make fun of your sibling's shortcomings. Focus on your own. Learn how to be supportive, rather than on putting others down. Guardian: Do not focus on your teen's shortcomings. Support them in their strengths—they already know their shortcomings.	Teen: You will create a hostile relationship between you and your siblings. This will give you an identity of being the "mean" sibling. Guardian: Teasing teens about their shortcomings and mistakes will create low self-esteem and feelings of not being "good enough" with your teen.

Ideas for Family Cleanup Activities

The purpose of family cleanup activities is to help the siblings who participated in disrespecting each other learn how to cooperate while working together on a task. It may take all day sitting with them during these tasks, but it is important that we see this consequence to its natural conclusion.

Jeff and Norm

Twins Jeff and Norm, now 17, used to be close—until they entered high school. Then they began the practice of taunting, teasing, demeaning, and hitting each other. Their parents, Marilyn and Henry, were at their wit's end. Every day was a new argument, with one or the other of them starting an altercation. The twin's parents just couldn't figure out what to do. They decided to try "family cleanup activities" as a way of having them learn about cooperation, negotiation, collaboration. Of course, Jeff and Norm could not have cared less about getting along with each other. Each got a charge out being irritating and teasing the other.

After considering their options regarding family cleanup activities, Marilyn and Henry drew up a contract much like the one above. They presented it to Jeff and Norm, who thought it was "hilarious," and advised their parents there was "no way" that they would participate in this "stupid idea."

Here's how it was presented:

"Jeff, Norm, we think that your constant arguing is having a negative effect on our family peace. We think we have been negligent in teaching you how to collaborate with and care about each other. If you were able to do that on your own, we wouldn't be worried that you will grow up and continue to bully and abuse each other both physically and emotionally. As your parents, we have decided that we need to intervene so you won't continue on this destructive path."

Norm and Jeff replied, "Whatever!!! We aren't abusing each other. You don't need to do anything! It's just fun."

Henry responded, "We know you feel that way or you wouldn't keep this disruptive behavior going on. So here's what's going to happen: The next time there is an argument between you two that erupts into one of you touching the other or taunting each other, we will have a 'family cleanup activity.'"

Jeff said, "That is the stupidest thing I have ever heard! I won't do it. That is so lame. You guys are weird."

Henry continued: "Yes we are, but we love you and we aren't going to let your disruptive behavior continue. I'm giving you each a list of family cleanup activities that your mother and I have agreed upon. Each activity is 30 minutes. If you get through the first activity without hitting each other or being disrespectful to each other, then you will have worked together and we can go on with our day. If, however, you argue, tease, swear, hit, or demean each other during that first family cleanup activity, then we will move on to the second activity and the third and fourth until you have worked together to complete the task. How long this takes is up to the two of you. Your mother and I will take turns watching you do the tasks. We don't care if it takes you all day and continues into the next. We are determined to help you learn what family love, cooperation, and respect is."

Norm became angry. "I'm not doing this! You can't make me!"

Marilyn answered, "That's up to you, but you will lose a belonging or privilege for each incident of being unwilling to participate in the family cleanup task. For example, the first time you refuse, you will lose your driving privileges for the week. The second time you decide not to cooperate, you will lose your cell phone for a week, then the door to your room, your computer, and so on. It is all up to you and your choices. Family kindness and respect is so important to your dad and me that we are willing to go to any lengths to teach this."

In a fury, Norm said, "You'll see! I'm not doing it! I refuse!" Then to Jeff he said, "And you, you little creep, this is entirely your fault!" Then Norm hit Jeff on the shoulder and Jeff hit him back. Marilyn and Henry looked at each other (and later shared their thought): "Oh God, we never thought we'd be tested so soon!"

Henry said, "Well, I guess you have decided that you really want to start this now. The first task is to wash your mom's car."

Jeff: "I'm not doing that, I have a date."

Norm: "I'm not doing that, I have football practice at 4:00" (it was 2:00).

Henry: "I see that you have time to wash your mom's car and still make it to your scheduled events. Let me know when you both want to start."

Norm turned to Jeff and said screamed, "This is your entire fault, you _ _ _ _ _ _ _!"

Henry calmly said, "I see we now have two cleanup activities. Let's see. My car also needs to be washed. That will take an hour for both activities if you two decide to cooperate and treat each other respectfully. Let me know when you want to start."

Henry knew he had his sons. Jeff wanted to go on his date, and Norm loved his football practices. Norm and Jeff turned to each other and guess what happened? They finished both cars in 45 minutes and they got along as they washed them!

Jeff and Norm tested their parent's resolve four more times, but Marilyn and Henry now have a much more peaceful existence with their teens.

Parents are to be present for these activities. Each activity is to last 30 minutes. They are to be done one after the other until siblings become cooperative with and respectful to each other. If completed before 30 minutes, it means your teens cooperated. While this may be inconvenient, it works! Parents are the judges of the quality of the cleanup activity. Remember, each task is to be done by at least two teens. They get to decide how to divide the task equitably.

Wash the car.

Wax the car.

Wash your neighbor's car.

Wax your neighbor's car.

Fold the wash.

Weed the garden for 30 minutes.

Weed your neighbor's garden for 30 minutes.

Clean up after the dog and put dirt containing grass seed over the brown spots in the lawn.

Walk the dog for 30 minutes.

Make every bed in the house.

Wash the dog.

Load/unload the dishwasher.

Sweep cobwebs off the entire house.

Stack wood for 30 minutes.

Wash the trash and recycling containers.

Wash the windows for 30 minutes.

Iron.

Clean a bathroom: the shower, toilet, sink, floor, mirror, etc.

On hands and knees, dust the hardwood floors.

Arrange newspapers/magazines in neat piles so it can be decided which go to recycling and which stay.

Plant a vegetable garden.

Water the yard.

Make up your own!

Consequences for Refusing Family Cleanup Activities

Your teens will test you at least once, so have a list of consequences for refusing family cleanup activities.

Here are some ideas:

> First refusal: Lose driving privileges for one week.
> Second refusal: Lose cell phone for one week.
> Third refusal: Door comes off bedroom.
> Fourth refusal: Video games are disconnected.
> Fifth refusal: Computer disconnected.
> Sixth refusal: Loss of a social activity.

Be creative. I've had teen patients who have lost their mattress, then their box springs, their TV, and so on. It is a test of wills and we caregivers need to win this one. One patient eventually worked his way into sleeping in the basement bathtub. He hated that so much he turned himself around.

The last option for sibling abuse is involving authority figures. A few times parents have had to call the police because their teen boys were hurting each other during their physical altercations. Don't be afraid to do this. Such abuse must be stopped!

The Loaning, Borrowing, and Losing of Personal Property

You just bought your teen a brand new Apple computer for his birthday. He loans it to his best friend, who accidently drops it. It now doesn't work.

Sally loves her tap shoes. She loans them to her best friend, who loses them.

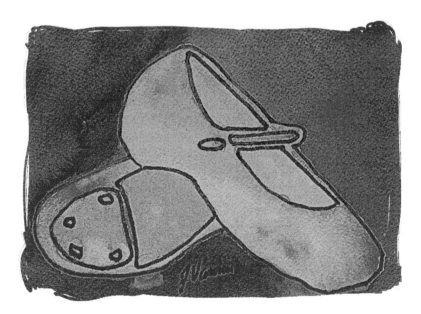

Peggy lets an acquaintance at school try on her new ring. Her friend won't return it.

These incidents are disheartening, irritating, and costly. We teach our teens to be generous, and it would seem natural for them to let their friends and acquaintances try out or try on some great acquisition. But accidents happen. "Friends" disappoint us. What can we guardians of teens do to help them determine if loaning a valued item to a friend is worth the risk of something happening to it. Or, how can we structure a lesson in valuing what one has? As we all know, there are some teens who have so much that they have little sustaining appreciation for their possessions.

The "loaning and losing of personal property" topic can provide us parents with an opportunity to instruct our teens how to weigh risks. It also delivers us caregivers with a chance to teach responsibility. Risk assessment is a valuable skill that can have far-reaching life benefits for your teen. What is risk assessment? In this case, it is thinking about if there is a danger of loss or destruction if we loan something to our teenage friend or acquaintance. It also allows teens to consider what would happen if they don't take care of and protect their possessions.

Here are ways to help us with risk versus benefit assessment:

1. Insignificant risk: I know my friend well and he is careful with his car and computer, so he'd probably be cautious if I let him borrow something. He wants to borrow my favorite CD overnight. He is responsible, and the item I'm loaning is of little monetary value because it was burned at home. I would feel upset if something happened to it but I can easily burn another one before I loan him mine. Benefit: I would feel good about letting him borrow my CD because he loves the music on it.

2. Minor risk: My friend has a 4-year-old sister who destroyed his computer. The little sister is visiting her out-of-state grandmother for a week. She isn't around. My pal wants to borrow my headphones because his grandma is sick and the TV disturbs her when she is trying to sleep. With my headphones, my pal could watch TV without waking his grandma. "Terminator Sister" won't be home. She could come home unexpectedly, but if that happens, my friend promised he will call me. The headphones cost $50. He and I talked to his parents, and they said they would buy me duplicates if anything happened to my headphones. Benefit: I could help out my pal.

3. Moderate risk: My best girlfriend wants to borrow my silver earrings because her brother stole hers. She is going out on a date, and she loves my earrings. My earrings have diamonds in them and cost $250. They were a gift from my grandma on my 17th birthday. I love them. I'm worried that my friend's brother will steal them like he stole hers, but my girlfriend is spending the night with a mutual pal of ours and promises to get the earrings back to me the next morning. The earrings are expensive. There is no agreed upon return time or about what happens if they are lost are stolen. Benefit: I would help out my friend and she would really appreciate it. In the past she has been trustworthy with stuff she has borrowed.

4. Major risk: Gary, my weed supplier, needs to borrow my new Apple computer for a week to help him with his pot-selling business. He wants to set up accounts on my computer, and when he gets enough money he will buy his own Apple and transfer his work there. Major risk: There is no return date. The Apple computer cost $2500. There is no agreement about replacement if the Apple is lost or damaged. Benefit: I would feel good about loaning Gary my computer. He has given me so much free weed and he will keep giving it to me if I can do him this favor.

The following is a template that parents and teens can do together to help them make decisions about whether it is a good idea to loan a piece of personal property. Teens have been known to loan their cars to other teens! Working on risk assessment with your teen can teach them to make prudent decisions now and throughout their life.

Determining Risk Worksheet

Deciding What Type of Risk Is Being Contemplated

Name of the item: _____

Cost of the item:

$1.00 – $10.00	_____	1 point
$10.01 – $20.00	_____	2 points
$20.01 – $100.00	_____	3 points
Over $100.00	_____	4 points

Do I have the money to replace the item?	Yes: _____ 0 points	No: _____ 8 points
Do I care about the item?	Yes: _____ 3 points	No: _____ 0 points
Does anyone co-own the item with me?	Yes: _____ 5 points	No: _____ 0 points
Does the co-owner know I will be lending this item?	Yes: _____ 3 points	No: _____ 10 points
Am I being pressured to loan this item?	Yes: _____ 10 points	No: _____ 0 points

Who is borrowing this item?

Good friend:	_____	3 points
Adult relative:	_____	3 points
School pal	_____	5 points
Acquaintance:	_____	10 points
Someone I barely know:	_____	10 points

Trustworthiness of the borrower:

Highly trustworthy:	_____	0 points
Moderately trustworthy:	_____	5 points
Do not know or not trustworthy:	_____	10 points

Do I have a written agreement?	Yes: _____ 3 points	No: _____ 10 points
Do I have a date and time of return?	Yes: _____ 3 points	No: _____ 10 points
Do parents know about this loan?	Yes: _____ 3 points	No: _____ 10 points

Is there an agreement about what happens if the borrowed item is not returned?
in the condition in which it was loaned? Yes: _____ 3 points   No: _____ 10 points

Total your score: _____

<u>Evaluate Your Score:</u>

1–15	Insignificant Risk
16–25	Minor Risk
26–50	Moderate Risk
51–100	Major Risk

Loaning and Borrowing Contract

Agreements	My Responsibilities	Consequences for Breaking Agreements
As your guardians, we want to give you items that make your life easier. We request that you do not loan expensive items.	Teen: Take good care of the items that make your life easier or fun such as computers, cell phones, a car, video games, etc. Do not loan anything that costs over $100. Guardian: Do NOT replace anything that is loaned and not returned for whatever reason.	Teen: The item you loan that is returned broken, or not returned at all, will not be replaced. YOU will have to earn the money to replace it. Guardian: If you dishonor this agreement you are teaching your teen that respect for their personal property is not really necessary. Even if you can afford to replace the loaned item, money is not the issue here.
As your guardians, we cannot be responsible for items you borrow from others. We request you do not borrow other people's property.	Teen: Do not borrow other people's belongings unless you know you have the money to replace it should it be damaged, lost, or stolen, whether or not it's your "fault." Guardian: How to replace the item that your teen borrowed and either got stolen, got damaged, or got lost, is NOT your problem. Resist all temptation to fix this for your teen.	Teen: If a borrowed item is damaged, stolen, or lost, I will be the one responsible for replacing it for the person I borrowed it from. Guardian: Paying for or replacing the item your teen borrowed teaches your teen that you will bail him/her out of the consequences that come from not evaluating a risk.
Teen: Acknowledges that if he/she decides to borrow or loan personal belongings, it is their responsibility to pay for any loss, damage to, or theft of the borrowed item.	Teen: Earn the money necessary to pay for the lost, damaged, or stolen item that was borrowed. To do this I will schedule "work details" with my guardian, neighbors, etc. Guardian: Sit with teen and discuss jobs to be done and the price to be paid for the completion of each task.	Teen: If you decide to not work to pay back the person you borrowed from, car insurance, allowance, cell phone fees, or Internet access (all monthly expenditures that add comfort to your life) will be canceled until the money saved from canceling these adds up to the price of the item that needs to be replaced. Guardian: A missed opportunity to teach your teen responsibility and respect for other people's property. Allowing a teenager's poor decisions to become YOUR responsibility.
Paying back debt: The borrower of an item has the responsibility of paying the cost of any lost, damaged, or stolen borrowed item.	Teen: Arrange a payment plan with the owner (and the owner's parents, when possible) of the borrowed item. Get a receipt for each payment. Make copies— one for you and one for your guardian.	Teen: You will have no proof of payment. Small claims court is a way owners of lost, damaged, stolen property can seek compensation. You might find yourself there.
Contracts for loaned/borrowed items to be signed by both parties—the borrower and the person who is loaning a personal belonging.	Teen: Make sure you have a contract when borrowing or loaning property. See Appendix C.	Teen: No contract? Then it is your word against the other person's. There is no one to believe. This will be your choice.

CHAPTER 6

You Now Have a Cell Phone!

I have a cell phone!

It seems like everyone over the age of five wants a cell phone. We take photos on them, play games on them, video call, search the Web, use a GPS system on them, and often they are a place to store the dates of birthdays and special events. But what about the temptations to abuse the privilege of having a cell phone?

We have all heard stories of how teens and young adults abuse a cell phone privilege. What often happens is that inordinate amounts of time are spent talking to and texting friends. Sometimes, sexting becomes an issue, wherein one takes a photo of an intimate part of one's body and sends it to a friend. Most parents don't want their offspring to participate in this type of activity. Most parents become angry about some aspect of cell phone use, such as overages. It is important to have a cell phone contract so each party knows the expectations of the other.

Having a cell phone is a privilege. Sometimes, parents' need to know the location of a cell phone holder provides them with a rationale for excusing irresponsible behavior with the phone. We cannot teach irresponsibility! We cannot teach lack of regard for a privilege. There are many ways to solve the need to know where the cell phone holder is, without giving a pass to taking one's cell phone for granted. If your cell phone contract is broken, one can procure a phone that only allows incoming calls. That way, if the whereabouts of your teen/young adult is of a concern, parents will have a way of connecting.

Gaming, texting, talking, and sending photos have become part of the teenage culture. This often keeps our next generation from developing interpersonal skills. Time limits on phone use assists in fostering one's teen to partake in one-on-one conversation. If they can't communicate via their cell, chances are getting together might be a necessary alternative.

Sexting has to have consequences. It denigrates the person who sends intimate photos. Sexting can have far-reaching and humiliating consequences. Incorporate this topic into your contract.

Cell Phone Contract: Parents Pay

Agreements	My Responsibilities	Consequences for Breaking Agreements
Parents will pay basic monthly phone bill.	<u>Teen</u>: Stay within the usage parameters.	If the holder of the cell phone goes over the allotted cell phone time and can't pay the difference between the basic bill and the overage charges, then use of the phone will be terminated until the overage bill is paid.
	Loss of Cell Phone <u>Teen</u>: Be mindful about the location of your cell phone so it doesn't get lost.	You get one cell phone. Loss of the phone results in YOU having to make arrangements for a prepaid phone. All parental responsibility will end.
	Theft of Cell Phone <u>Teen</u>: File a police report. Tell parents. <u>Parents</u>: Purchase theft/loss insurance through your local provider.	<u>Teen</u>: If a police report is not filed, AND if parents are not notified about a cell phone theft, the privilege of having a cell phone is lost for six months. Theft is a criminal offense and must be reported.
	Time Limits of Cell Use <u>Teen</u>: For 30 minutes after dinner, I will be allowed to communicate with friends on my phone. This will be AFTER my homework/job duties are completed.	<u>Teen</u>: Violation of the time limits set in this contract will result in loss of the cell phone privilege for the next 24 hours.
	Lending One's Cell Phone <u>Teen</u>: Keep my cell phone in my possession and do not loan it to anyone.	Any loss/damage to one's phone due to lending it will be the financial responsibility of the teen .

Signed: _____   Signed: _____

Date: _____   Date: _____

Just because your young adult is paying for a cell phone doesn't make him exempt from parental structure around cell phone use. Even if your teen is over 18, if he/she is living in your house, YOU, the guardian and provider of room and board, still have the ability to have influence. When someone is living in your house, YOU have every right to expect your home rules to be respected, regardless of who is paying for which service.

It is true, once your young adult is self-supporting, and living on his own, our parental controls end. If we have done our job as caregivers, our teens will have knowledge of acceptable behavior. If they decide to violate the values with which they have been raised, then that becomes their choice and their consequences.

This agreement is intended for young adults (over 18) living at home, job or no job.

Cell Phone Contract: Teen Pays

Agreements	My Responsibilities	Consequences for Breaking Agreements
It is the family's expectation that young adult will use cell phone in a responsible way: no sexting, and no bullying of others.	Young Adult: Will use their cell phone appropriately. What that means is that no adult would be offended by the contents of texts, emails, and social media.	Parents: If it comes to our attention that how you are using your phone is disrespectful to yourself or others, you will forfeit use of your cell phone for one week. We reserve the right to check your cell phone.
Cell phones are to be off during meals. There is no leaving the table to make a call.	Young Adult: Make sure my cell phone is either turned off or in another room during meals. Parents: Follow the same expectations you have for your teen regarding cell phone use at mealtime.	Teen: Loss of cell phone use the next day. Parents: Loss of cell phone use the next day. (We parents are NOT exempt from family agreements.)
Parents are not responsible for loss or theft of young adult's cell phone. Each carrier has plans that are available for an extra monthly charge that protects against loss, damage, or theft.	Young Adult: Investigate the cost of extra insurance and decide if it is worth it to you to pay for that added protection against damage, loss, or theft.	Young Adult: Not having a cell phone.
Texting while driving is prohibited.	Young Adult: Drive safely and do not respond to texts when behind the wheel.	Young Adult: Loss of driving privileges and cell phone for one week.
Young Adult: Cell phone may be used after homework is completed for one hour per night.	Young Adult: Monitor yourself. Parents: Will not monitor you. When you go over an hour, you are selecting the consequence.	Young Adult: Loss of cell phone for one week.

CHAPTER 7

Teens and Young Adults Living at Home

Living at Home With a Job

Now your teen is 18, and a legal adult. They have graduated from high school and don't want to further their education right now. They want a job and some rest from academics. And let's face it, some of the motivation behind such a decision might be that your young adult simply wants to PARTY!

Here they are a legal adult, living in your house, eating your food, and holding down a job, and most often your young adult will think, "All the rules of this household that applied to me, no longer apply because I'm a legal adult!" This attitude can lead to major problems. Watch out! If you don't get a handle on this attitude, chaos, arguments, and other kinds of abhorrent behavior might walk through your front door.

It is crucial to have an agreement regarding guidelines for continuing to live in the home of one's parents. It is only fair to let your young adult know your expectations. This will eliminate many arguments in the future. And always remember, if your young adult doesn't like your home structure, they are free to move out. It is totally their decision. THEY are living with YOU.

The suggested agreements below are not about trying to control your teen. They are about avoiding chaos in your home. Parents are entitled to live a life independent of their adult offspring. Parents have a right to establish a home structure that is comfortable for them. If caregivers hand over the reins of the house to their young adult, they are placing too much responsibility on them. Teens need structure. It provides a foundation for having the ability to organize one's own life.

The suggestion of eviction in the sample contract is meant to let your young adult know that you are serious about guideline compliance. The 12-point system was designed so that the teen, as well as the parents, know how many contract violations have to be earned before the living arrangements need to be changed. This is all up to your young adult. A 30-day eviction notice can be found online or at your local board of Realtors or in Appendix A in this book. Get one. Show it to your teen. Let them know that you are serious about the responsibilities of those who reside in your home.

It is also necessary to define exactly what entitlements come from paying rent. Paying rent means that the young adult has use of their bedroom and a bathroom, and the other comforts of your home. It does NOT mean that they have freedom from complying with any other home rules. It does NOT mean that they can live in your home in a manner that contradicts the preferences of the caregivers. For example, if parents live in a clean and tidy home, just because their adult offspring pays rent doesn't entitle them to keep their living space looking like a pigpen. With or without telling them, many parents put the rent money into a savings account for their young adult. The money is often returned for a special event such as leaving for college, or for a security deposit on an apartment, a wedding, the birth of a child, etc.

Ever watch the movie *Failure to Launch*? I invite you to watch it. We do not want to debilitate our young adults. We do not want to provide the services of a hotel to our teens while they live at home. To live at home while one works is a privilege, not a right. In a loving way, foster the idea that living on one's own is the goal and manifestation of being an adult.

Living at Home With a Job Contract

Agreements	My Responsibilities	Consequences for Breaking Agreements
Curfew: 11:00 P.M. weekdays, 1:00 A.M. Friday and Saturday.	Teen: Be home on time. There is no flexibility in contract for lateness.	Teen: For every infraction, the rent increases by $10, due from the next paycheck.
Parents: Decide what the drugs and alcohol policy is at your home. Write it down. Give it to your teen.	**Drugs/Alcohol** Parents: For those under the age of 21, is there a tolerance for drug/alcohol use in this family? (If not, decide if there are any exceptions to this, such as wine at dinner on holidays, etc.). In most states, it is against the law to drink under the age of 21. Decide if it is against your family values. For those 21 and over, decide what is tolerable for you. Can friends drink at your house? What about marijuana use at your house?	Teen: If there are incidents wherein you come home in an intoxicated state, a protocol of home drug testing will be established. For entry into the house, you will have to test on demand. The number of incidents of coming home intoxicated/high will be determined by parents and the young adult will be advised of that number. (Incorporate it into this contract.) For example: "We know you drink, but for the last two nights you have come home drunk. One more time and we will begin drug testing you."
Friends are allowed to visit when the parents are at home.	Teen: Be sure my friends respect the property of my parents and abide by home guidelines. Parents: Specify which friends are welcome in your home and when.	Teen: Having friends over when parents are not home will result in the earning of 3 points toward eviction.
Young adult is to pay $200 per month as rent.	**Rent** To pay $100 out of each paycheck if you are paid bimonthly.	Earning 3 points toward the eviction notice and a $15 late fee.
30 day notice (See Appendix A: Sample 30-Day Notice to Quit.)	Teen: Comply with the contract so you can continue to live in the home. Eviction has a 12-point limit per month. Upon reaching the twelfth point, an eviction notice will be given to the young adult stipulating that you are being given notice that you have to vacate the premise in 30 days. The eviction notice is irrevocable.	Leaving the family living situation. This is totally the teen's choice, since they have been given fair notice about the terms of their living in the family home.

College Vacations

When our young adults come home for vacation during a college break, they often expect their parents to adjust to the lifestyles they have adopted while away from home. All those late-night hours, parties, having myriad people their age to talk to, and being able to come and go as they desire often leads to feeling an entitlement to continue their college lifestyle at home. This can be very disruptive!

Parents: Decide what you expect from your college student while he/she is home. Do you want to allow your young adult to "party hearty" during their break? Are they underage? What limits will you need to set? BE AWARE! Many college students drink and smoke marijuana while away from home. What are your home rules about that? Can your college student sleep all day? Is it OK to watch TV or play video games all day? Teens might rationalize such behavior by advising their parents that it's their vacation, and they can "do whatever I want."

The college vacation contract is more about letting your college student know what the parental expectations are. Having a written agreement allows your young adult to know how to proceed while vacationing at home.

Living at Home During College Vacations Contract

Agreements	My Responsibilities	Consequences for Breaking Agreements
No drinking and driving.	Teen: Call parents/taxi for a ride home when drinking. Parents will gladly pick up teen. However, there may be other consequences for getting so impaired that one can't drive.	Teen: This is a serious infraction. Drinking and driving puts you and others at risk. It also shows extremely poor judgment. For first infraction, no use of the car for three weeks. If there is a second infraction, use of the car while at college may be limited or denied.
Curfew is 1:00 A.M. each night of the week. No disruption of other people's sleep.	Teen: Make sure you are prompt. Do not disrupt the sleep of members of the family.	Teen: For each minute late, the curfew for the following day will be diminished by one hour.
Sleep	Teen: Is to arise by 10:00 A.M. each day.	For each minute over the "rise and shine time," curfew that day will be diminished by one hour.
Friends	Teen: May invite friends over when parents are home, and with parent's permission. Parents: Will order pizza or provide food and soft drinks for teen's guests.	Teen: No use of drugs or alcohol will be allowed in the home. Over 21: Friends may bring their own alcohol into the house and drink it in a responsible manner. No use of marijuana or other drugs on the premise.
We love you to come home.	Teen: Have fun while at home.	Teen: Your fun is up to you.

Barry

Barry just finished his first semester at college. He did very well, and earned a 3.5 GPA. Barry's family was extremely proud of their son, and excited to have him come home for Chanukah. Barry asked his mother and grandmother if they would mind if he brought home a couple of college friends for the holiday. One friend wanted to learn what it was like to celebrate Chanukah. The other friend's parents were going to be in Europe for the holiday, and Barry thought it would be nice for him not to spend that time alone in the dorm.

Barry's mom and grandmother were delighted to open their home to Barry's new friends. When they arrived at Barry's house, they seemed polite, respectful, and like "great guys," to quote Barry's mother. They arrived with duffel bags full of clothes and personal hygiene items. All three teens were going to stay in Barry's room because he had two twin beds, and his room could accommodate an air mattress that his mom and grandmother had for guests.

Barry also had a 15-year-old brother and a 14-year-old sister. They thought it was "too kewl," to have Barry's college friends come home to help celebrate Chanukah. Barry's sister thought one of Barry's new pals was "very handsome and funny." His brother also liked Barry's friends. At dinner Barry's grandmother and mom thought that Barry and his friends were very entertaining in how they recounted events they had shared at college. A great time was had by all.

Then came bedtime! Barry and his friends were up all night, talking, laughing, and playing computer games. Of course, this kept Barry's mom and grandmother up all night as well. In the morning, when his mom and grandmother had to get up to tend to their responsibilities, Barry and his pals slept in until 1:00 in the afternoon! The next evening, while Mom and Grandma were exhausted, Barry and his pals were all ready to replay the fun they had the previous evening. Mom and Grandma were becoming irritated and resentful. They thought that Barry and his guests were being inconsiderate of them and their work schedules. Barry and his pals were oblivious to the needs of their hosts.

The third day into Barry's holiday at home, his mother and grandmother took him aside and told him how angry they were; they felt disrespected, discounted, taken advantage of, etc. And Barry, for his part, was shocked that his caregivers wanted to put limits on his "fun" during his vacation! Barry felt he had earned his vacation by doing well in school, and that his caregivers weren't acknowledging all his hard work by allowing him a "no house rules" vacation break at home.

Before your young adult leaves for college, make an agreement for what is expected of him/her during holiday vacations, and when they bring friends home from school for short stays. It is only fair to let your teen know your expectations, otherwise, you, the parent, sets him/her up for altercation.

Living at Home While Attending College

Having teens live at home while they attend college can be a joy or an issue. Students need to know what is expected of them in order to live at home. When our teens enter college, parents often relax expectations. However, no matter how lax behavioral guidelines become, your young adult still needs to know what the limits are of living in your home.

Are you going to provide "hotel service" by washing and ironing clothes for your young adult? By cooking meals? Does it matter how messy their room is? Think about these things. You now have a legal adult living in your home. If you allow adolescent behavior, then you are not only sending a covert message that this is acceptable, but you are enabling your teen to remain dependent on his/her parent(s). The Living at Home While Attending College Contract is much different than the College Contract because it addresses actual living standards.

Janice

Janice was a "B" student in high school. Her parents believed that education was the only thing that Janice should focus on while she was in high school, so Janice had no responsibilities at home. Her mother cleaned her room, laundered her clothes, packed a school lunch for her, and prepared breakfast and dinner. All Janice had to do was study.

After high school graduation, it was decided that Janice would continue to live at home while attending junior college for two years. Janice expected that her parents would continue on as they had during her time in high school. She also expected that she would have more freedom to come and go as she pleased since she was now in college.

Over the summer break between high school and college, Janice's mother discovered that she was tired of waiting on Janice. Her mother had gotten a part-time job and didn't have time to tend to her daughter as she previously had. She developed resentments that her daughter didn't pitch in and keep her own room tidy and didn't pick up after herself when she used the kitchen. Her mother felt disrespected when Janice asked her where her clean jeans were.

Things were about to change for Janice. Janice's parents had a conversation about their daughter taking for granted all the comforts of her home. They found that they had trained their daughter to regard them as waiters and waitresses, doing her bidding. They discovered that Janice had no feeling of her family being a community that needed participation from each of its members to keep it going.

Janice's parents presented her with a contract. It delineated the new ways that Janice would have to participate in the family to be able to remain in her home. At first, Janice was irate! When she found that her parents were nonnegotiable, she grudgingly complied. For about a month, there were many upsets. When Janice's hairspray disappeared from the bathroom counter, she was furious. When her favorite jeans were donated to a charity because they had been left on the middle of her bedroom floor, she had a tantrum. Eventually, however, Janice learned that in order to stay in her house as a college student, she had responsibilities. Over time, she felt more connected with her family because she was a participating member who contributed to the smooth running of her house.

Living at Home While Attending College Contract

Agreements	My Responsibilities	Consequences for Breaking Agreements
	Kitchen Student: Used dishes put in the dishwasher. Food put away. Counters kept clean.	Student: Loss of kitchen privileges for the day following. Parents: Cleaning up after your adult student makes this contract null and void.
	Minimal "C" GPA Student: Attend classes and keep a GPA of 2.0. College is your JOB. You have to show up and perform.	Student: Two consecutive semesters/quarters of grades lower than a 2.0 GPA will result in you having to move out of the house and support yourself. Parents: Creating a dependency relationship wherein your student is relieved from the responsibility of doing his/her job without consequences.
	Laundry Student: Is responsible for his/her own laundry and freeing the washer and dryer from clean clothes so others can use the equipment.	Student: Clothes left in the dryer shall be stored in a safe place for one week. Two infractions per week, student will have to wash and dry clothes in public facilities for the following week.
	Living Conditions Student: Is required to keep your living spaces clean and free from debris. Bed is made on a daily basis, and countertops in the bathroom are cleared of personal items before leaving the house.	Student: Everything left on the bathroom counter shall be thrown away. You will have to find the money to replace them. Clothes left on the bedroom floor shall be donated to a charity.
	Curfew Student: Must be home by 11:00 P.M. on weekdays, and 1:00 A.M. on weekends.	Student: Curfew violations will result in being awakened the next day by the amount of time one was past curfew. This means being out of bed. Noncompliance leads to loss of cell phone for one day.

Living at Home Without a Job

Your teen has graduated from high school! Three months have passed and you have watched him live each day the same: Sleep until noon, get up, shower, eat, play video games, eat, go out with friends, come home at 3:00 A.M., and the cycle continues. Your teen says he's just recuperating from going to high school. He tells you he deserves to have some fun with his pals. How long is he planning on continuing this lifestyle?

YOU, as his parent and as his chief provider, get to determine this. If you continue to allow your young adult to hang out at home with no responsibilities and no plans for his future, YOU are covertly delivering the message that this is acceptable behavior! Is that really what you intended?

Joe

Joe lived with his single mother in a home that was left to her, free and clear, by Joe's maternal grandmother. His mother, Brenda, liked it when Joe was home, because she felt safer having a "man" around the house. When Joe graduated from high school, he had no idea of what to do for a career. He was accustomed to being with his high school buddies, playing basketball, hanging out, and having little structure to his life. Brenda occasionally did ask Joe if he thought he should get a job, and Joe would agree with her after complaining about the job market and his inability to find work, "even though I've looked."

Joe lived with his mother through his twenties. Then he lived with his mother through his thirties. When Brenda's friends and the rest of Joe's family inquired about what Joe was doing to make a living, Brenda would tell them that he was taking care of the yard and the house for her. Then Joe found a girlfriend. He spent much time with her at her apartment. For one year, Joe wasn't home very much, until one day he showed up very upset. His girlfriend had accused him of living off her and had kicked him out. Brenda was happy to have him home.

Joe lived with his mother through his forties and fifties. In his forties, he began to drink and spent much time at a bar. Brenda worried about him, but the idea of not having Joe with her was untenable. And then Brenda died. She left Joe the house, her car, a life insurance policy worth $50,000, and all her bills. Joe had no idea what to do. He had been living off his mother for so long, he had become dependent. Joe continued to drink and ignore the real estate taxes, his mother's bills, and any other debts. Eventually, Joe lost his entire inheritance and became homeless. Currently, Joe lives under a freeway overpass in California. He cannot see his way to other options. He is a victim of learned helplessness. Joe had a mother who put her needs before her son's. Brenda helped create an adult who never individuated and never earned a sense of self or a sense of accomplishment.

After high school graduation, a young adult needs to structure his days. He needs to have some responsibilities in order to learn how to support himself. Approach your teen. Discover what his plan is for the near future. If he doesn't have one, YOU get to put one in motion. Returning to school or applying for an apprenticeship are great ideas that require footwork on the part of the teen. For college, getting the class catalog from the local community college is a first step. For an apprenticeship, contacting trade unions is a way to discover how to get training.

The following contract provides some ideas about how to direct the jobless teen.

Contract: Living at Home Without a Job

Agreements	My Responsibilities	Consequences for Breaking Agreements
Teen: May have two weeks after high school graduation to socialize with friends, be lazy, and rest.	Teen: Have fun in line with family values and other contracts in place.	Teen: Selecting NOT to have fun due to consequences in other contracts, e.g., Car Contract, Prom Contract.
Beginning week 3, teen is to start looking for a job. Teen: Has from week 3 to week 8 after graduation to be hired. Parent: Respect your teen by honoring his/her ability to find a job.	Teen: Find a job Parent: If asked, parent to help with ideas. Do NOT nag, remind, encourage, or get involved with your teen's job search. This is your teen's responsibility.	Teen: Being given a 30-day notice to vacate the family home if a job is not procured by week 8 after graduation. A 30-day notice means that you have an additional 30 days to find a job, but by day 30, you are to be moved out should you not find a job—this does NOT mean a promise of a job; it means actual employment. Parent: Not enforcing a 30-day notice gives your teen the message that you don't mean what you say. (See Appendix A: Sample 30-Day Notice to Quit.)
Teen: Upon finding a job, 25% of your income will be contributed to the household for room and board. Parent: Implement a written rental agreement that describes late fees, responsibilities of landlord and tenant.	Teen: Be diligent in delivering your rent to your parents by the due date. Parent: Abide by the rental agreement without grace periods.	Teen: For not abiding by the rental agreement, you will be given a 30-day notice to vacate the premises. Parent: Forgiving lateness or late fees for breach of your rental agreement will teach your teen that you don't respect your rental agreement and neither will your teen.
Teen: If you determine that you need more training for a job, make a proposal to your parents, IN WRITING.	Teen: Make a detailed plan about how you propose to get more job training. (Returning to school and naming the courses you will take is usually welcomed by parents. Also applying for apprenticeships is a way to get job training.) Parent: Listen to your teen's proposal, without judgment. Ask for more details if you feel the plan is too vague.	Teen: By not determining a career, you risk being homeless three months after graduation from high school! Parent: By allowing your teen to remain home indefinitely without a job, you are creating a dependency that, in the long run, could incapacitate your teen.
Teen: Once you have a job, be on time, be a good employee, explore if this job is what you want to do for the rest of your life. If not, get training for another job.	Teen: Keep your job. If you determine you don't like this job, look for another one BEFORE you quit the job you have. Parent: Listen to teen's thoughts about his/her job.	Teen: You will still be responsible for your rent. Failure to pay it will result in a 30-day notice after two months. Parent: If you allow your teen to live with you rent free, there is little incentive for your teen to get a job.

Know Your Values

Good parenting requires the parent to know specifically, what is "OK" and what is "not OK" behavior. It is crucial that each family knows what their values are. Family values are what provide the structure for rules of engagement, behavior, academics, relationships, and careers. Without family values, children, teens, and young adults can easily get lost in the morass of choices about how to engage with others, what is meaningful in life, and how to acclimate themselves to society.

The following can be a very fun exercise for parents to do with children, teens, and young adults. Get a sheet of paper and put three vertical columns on it. Label the header on the first column "Most Important Values." At the top of the second column put the title "Somewhat Important Values." Title the third column "Unimportant Values."

Select one person to read the list of values on the following page. This exercise is not meant to provide time to consider the values for a prolonged period. They must be read at a slow enough pace to allow them to be written down, but quick enough to disallow time for thought before making your choice. The values are in no particular order. The goal is to put into words, the instinctive values that we hold. Knowing our values will help provide a structure for our family. A blank template is in Appendix D.

Example

Most Important Values	Somewhat Important Values	Unimportant Values
Friendship	Solitude	Fitness
Generosity	Beauty	Accuracy
Stability	Romance	Risk

"It's not hard to make decisions, once you know what your values are."
~ Roy E. Disney

List of Values

Acceptance – to be accepted as I am

Accuracy – to be accurate in my opinions and beliefs

Achievement – to have important accomplishments

Adaptability – the ability to adjust oneself readily to different conditions

Adventure – to have new and exciting experiences

Attractiveness – to be physically attractive

Authority – to be in charge of and responsible for others

Autonomy – to be self-determined and independent

Beauty – to appreciate beauty around me

Caring – to take care of others

Challenge – to take on difficult tasks and problems

Change – to have a life full of change and variety

Comfort – to have a pleasant and comfortable life

Commitment – to make enduring, meaningful commitments

Compassion – to feel and act on concern for others

Contribution – to make a lasting contribution in the world

Cooperation – to work collaboratively with others

Courtesy – to be considerate and polite toward others

Creativity – to have new and original ideas

Curiosity – a strong desire to know or learn something

Dependability – to be reliable and trustworthy

Duty – to carry out my duties and obligations

Ecology – to live in harmony with the environment

Excitement – to have a life full of thrills and stimulation

Faithfulness – to be loyal and true in relationships

Fame – to be known and recognized

Family – to have a happy, loving family

Fitness – to be physically fit and strong

Flexibility – to adjust to new circumstances

Forgiveness – to be forgiving of others

Friendship – to have close, supportive friends

Fun – to play and have fun

Generosity – to give what I have to others

Genuineness – to act in a manner that is true to who I am

God's will – to seek and obey the will of God

Growth – to keep changing and growing

Health – to be physically well and healthy

Helpfulness – to be supportive of others
Honesty – to be honest and truthful
Hope – to maintain a positive and optimistic outlook
Humility – to be modest and unassuming
Humor – to see the humorous side of myself and the world
Independence – to be free from dependence on others
Industry – to work hard and well at my life tasks
Inner peace – to experience personal peace
Intimacy – to have affectionate, close relationships
Justice – to promote fair and equal treatment for all
Knowledge – to learn and contribute valuable knowledge
Leisure – to take time to relax and enjoy
Loved – to be loved by those close to me
Loving – to give love to others
Mastery – to be competent in my everyday activities
Mindfulness – to live conscious and mindful of the present moment
Moderation – to avoid excesses and find a middle ground
Monogamy – to have one close, loving relationship
Nonconformity – to question and challenge authority and norms
Nurturance – to take care of and nurture others
Openness – to be open to new experiences, ideas, and options
Order – to have a life that is well-ordered and organized
Passion – to have deep feelings about ideas, activities, or people
Pleasure – to feel good
Popularity – to be well-liked by many people
Power – to have control over others
Purpose – to have meaning and direction in my life
Rationality – to be guided by reason and logic
Realism – to see and act realistically and practically
Responsibility – to make and carry out responsible decisions
Risk – to take risks and chances
Romance – to have intense, exciting love in my life
Safety – to be safe and secure
Self-acceptance – to accept myself as I am
Self-control – to be disciplined in my own actions
Self-esteem – to feel good about myself
Self-knowledge – to have a deep and honest understanding of myself
Service – to be of service to others
Sexuality – to have an active and satisfying sex life
Simplicity – to live life simply, with minimal needs

Solitude – to have time and space where I can be apart from others

Spirituality – to grow and mature spiritually

Stability – to have a life that stays fairly consistent

Tolerance – to accept and respect those who differ from me

Tradition – to follow respected patterns of the past

Virtue – to live a morally pure and excellent life

Wealth – to have plenty of money

World peace – to work to promote peace in the world.

Knowing your values will guide you in all decision making!

CHAPTER 8

I Can Drive!

Oh Dear, My Teen Can Drive

With teens and young adults, it is imperative to have a Car Contract so each party will know the responsibilities involved with the privilege of driving. This is actually the only fair and just way to manage teen driving. Otherwise, consequences are given when situations arise, and the new driver never gets to make decisions regarding if the "benefits" of engaging in bad driving judgments outweigh the consequences for bad decisions.

To illustrate the above point, if I am late for a college class, and I know that if I go 100 mph down the freeway, I will get to my class on time, I'd be very tempted to speed. However, if, at the same time, I also knew that getting a speeding ticket would ground me from driving to school and I'd have to take public transportation for a week and I'd have to come up with the money to pay the ticket or spend time in jail, I might think twice about any decision to speed. With a Car Contract in place, the choice that is made belongs to the young driver, NOT to his/her parents.

It is also important to have agreements about how a young adult procures a car. What is the path they need to follow in order to have their parents put themselves at risk by allowing their teen to drive? And parents, be aware that YOU are the ones responsible for all the decisions made by your underage driver or by any driver on your insurance policy. It is YOUR financial risk. Why would any parent ever put him/herself in the position of allowing their financial solvency to be jeopardized by their teen's driving decisions?

Because earning one's driver's license is a life milestone that many teens expect to reach, the privilege of driving needs to be approached in a step-by-step manner. First, one starts with the Car Contract for Driver's Permit and Driver's Education. This way, your teen will know the steps he/she must take in order to earn the privilege of driving. In this contract, address just who pays for the permit and for driver's education. While this may seem unnecessary, there are many families who are financially strapped, and the possibility of paying for one extra thing is nonexistent.

Next, parents need to determine what criteria will be used to allow the procurement of a driver's license. Does your teen need to have a "B" average in school before they can get their license? Do they need to be drug free for 60 days before their parents take them to the DMV to take their licensing test? Be very clear about what your teen needs to do in order for you, their caregiver, to facilitate them getting the privilege to drive. Don't make your criteria unreachable. This will only serve to create resentments about how one's parents make it impossible for them to achieve their goal of being able to drive.

From here, parents need to consider if their teen will be allowed to drive their car, or if their teen will have the opportunity to be given or earn a car of their own. Your teen deserves clarity on this subject. It is through the guidelines the parents create that their young driver will be able to make an informed choice.

Are there any other requirements for teens to have the privilege of having a driver's permit and for taking driver's education? If so, your teen needs to be informed of your expectations and to be advised of what their parents are willing to finance. One can gain a lot of leverage with a teen by setting up criteria for them to have to meet in order to get a permit and driver's education. Select one or two achievements they have to reach in order to earn the privilege to drive. Too many demands will only serve to overwhelm and extinguish any desire to participate in agreements with parents.

It used to be that public schools provided driver's education classes. Now, however, very few public schools fund driver's training. The expense falls on parents. In making the decision about if your teen is ready to have the responsibility of driving, one might start with the questions, "Is my teen responsible enough to be behind the wheel of a car?" "Is my teen trustworthy enough not to put him/herself in risky situations while he/she is driving?" Be honest with yourselves about the answers to these questions. Remember, you, the parents, *are financially liable for your teen's driving*. You are responsible for their safety and the safety of others. Think long and hard about if you trust your teen enough to put your financial security in his/her hands. Consider if giving your teen more time to mature would decrease the chances of your teen getting in high-risk situations with the car.

Car Contract for Driver's Permit: Parent/s Pay

Agreements	My Responsibilities	Consequences for Breaking Agreements
Teen: Earn a B- (2.7) GPA or higher the semester before requesting the privilege of getting a driver's permit.	Teen: Discuss grades with caregivers to substantiate your GPA. Provide written documentation from the school.	No driving permit.
Teen: Will research how to procure a driver's permit, and present the results to guardians.	Teen: Inform parents about what is needed from the DMV for you to get your permit. Parents: Will not do this research for teen.	No driving permit.
Teen: Will research driver's education classes and present parents with the information and cost for three of them.	Parents: Set aside time to discuss the results of teen's research. Select one of the options and include your teen in the discussion.	No driving permit. No driver's education classes.
Parents: Agree to pay for the cost of teen's driving permit and for the cost of driver's training.	Parents: Pay for this in a timely manner (within one week of teen's presentation of research about fees charged by the DMV and driver's training classes).	Teen will believe that parents are not reliable. Teen will believe that parents are not trustworthy. Teen will remember lack of parent's follow through as a betrayal. Long-term relationship consequences.
Parents: Will provide transportation to and from the DMV and to and from driver's training classes. Teen: Show up on time. Parents will not provide reminders for teen.	Parents: One week in advance, come to a mutual agreement about what time teen will be in the car for their ride to and from the DMV and driver's education classes. Add the time to this agreement.	Teen: Two times being late to the car for transportation, and this contract becomes null and void. Teen will have to wait one month to renegotiate this contract.

Rodney

Rodney loved to have a good time, and hang out with his pals. At 15, he couldn't wait to learn how to drive so he could participate in the thrill his friends experienced by playing high-risk driving games. Without his parent's knowledge, Rodney would sit shotgun in the cars of some of his pals while they engaged in dangerous, often life-threatening games. Often, Rodney's homies were high on weed or some other substance.

Rodney's favorite game was called "Assassins." This game involved speeding cars and water guns. Rodney's friends would drive around, chasing each other in their cars while squirting water guns out of the windows.

The game "Fugitive" was another exciting game, wherein drivers chase the "fugitives," who are running away from them. It is rather like "Hide and Go Seek," using a vehicle to hunt for and catch the group who has agreed to run away from the car. Once the "fugitives" are caught, the car is stopped abruptly, as in a high-speed chase, and the driver must then jump out of the car and chase the fugitives.

"Drifting" was the scariest for Rodney, but he still participated in it, lest his buddies would think he was a "chicken" if he didn't. In the "Drifting" game, the driver purposely forces the rear wheels of the car to lose traction. This causes the car to move sideways along a curve. Without great skill from the driver, the drifting car can easily spin out of control and over the side of the road.

Rodney's parents were not aware of their son's propensity for thrill-seeking activities in the cars of his friends. When their 15-year-old was gone during the evening, he had told them he was playing video games at the house of one of his buddies. Rodney's parents never checked.

Rodney and his parents awaited the day when he got his driver's permit and learned to drive. This would provide some independence for them. Their son would be able to drive himself to and from school as well as maybe run an occasional errand for them. As an extra bonus, perhaps Rodney would be able to drive his little sister to her dance class.

On the day he turned 15½, Rodney got his permit and the next day he began driver's training. At the end of his classes, Rodney's best friend thought he'd give Rodney a chance to drive during an "Assassin" game. Rodney was thrilled! At last! He could be one of the guys. It didn't matter that he wasn't licensed. It didn't matter that he had no driving experience except through driver's training and the few times his mother had let him drive her to appointments.

So Rodney got behind the wheels of his friend's car. While trying to catch up with an opponent's car in order to squirt them, Rodney lost control and ran his friend's car into the shrubbery of someone's house. There was damage to his friend's car, and damage to the property of the homeowner. Guess who had to pay for their 15½-year-old's poor judgment? Guess who decided their son wasn't mature enough to be trusted to drive in a safe manner? His parents!

Guess who didn't get his driver's license until his 18th birthday? You guessed it! Rodney!

Parent and Teen Financial Participation

Collaborating with one's teen about how to pay for learning how to drive can provide a bonding moment. As in the story of Mary (below), planning for such an event that is so meaningful to one's teen provides an opportunity for the parent to role-model how to work out a plan for reaching a goal beforehand. It also provides a teen's caretaker(s) a chance to role-model financial responsibility, how to save for something one wants, and how to have patience when working toward a goal.

Car Contract for Driver's Permit and Driver's Education

Agreements	My Responsibilities	Consequences for Breaking Agreements
Teen: Will research the costs of obtaining a driver's permit and the price of three different driver's education courses (to shop for the best deal).	Teen: Give computer-researched costs results to parents for their consideration.	No driving permit or driver's education classes.
Teen and Caretaker(s): Will meet to discuss findings. Teen will arrange the date and time for such meeting. Caregivers(s) will make themselves available.	Teen: Arrange a meeting time. Caregivers(s): be flexible and available to discuss teen's research.	Teen: No driving permit or driver's education classes. Parent(s): Teaching their teen that they are unreliable in the area of carrying out agreements. This has far-reaching consequences concerning trust.
Caregiver(s): Will pay half of the cost of a driving permit and of driver's education classes when teen turns 15½. Teen: Must maintain a 2.8 GPA or higher in school for the semester prior to obtaining the permit and driving instruction.	Caregiver(s): Discuss and show teen how you are saving to pay for your part of this agreement. Teen: Attend school, do your homework, and study for tests.	Lack of positive consequences, namely: Caregiver(s): Teaching your teen how to be financially responsible. Teen: Earning a privilege provides self-esteem and increases self-confidence.
Teen: Will pay the remaining half of driving permit and of driver's education classes.	Teen: Research and discuss with caregiver(s) ways of earning money, and follow through on them. Establish a savings account at your local bank.	No driving permit or driver's education classes.
Caregiver(s): Will accompany teen to interview potential employers and to assist teen in negotiating a price for services rendered.	Caregiver(s): Keep teen out of potentially unsafe situations. Role-model for teen how to negotiate for pay.	Caregiver(s): Teen could be at risk when signing up to work for an unknown person. Teen does not have the skill to screen for safety.

Mary

At 15½, Mary looked forward to the day she could drive. She couldn't wait to be able to have her own transportation and be able to go places without her parents having to take her. The idea of being able to turn up the car stereo and blast her favorite music seemed like the pinnacle of "kewlness."

Mary approached her mom about getting her driving permit. Her mother agreed to sign the necessary papers and take Mary to the DMV to fill out the application forms. Mary was so excited when she received her permit! She couldn't wait to take driver's training so she could get her license. But Mary's mother was having financial difficulties, and couldn't afford the cost of driver's training. Mary became enraged because she had expected her mother to pay for her to learn how to drive.

Mary began to act out. She refused to do any of her jobs around the house. She refused to study. Her grades plummeted. Mary felt that her mother should have let her know about her inability to pay for the requisites she needed to drive a vehicle.

If Mary's mother had been candid and collaborated with her about how to earn the money for a driver's education course, this situation could have been avoided. If Mary's mother had sat her down and advised her that she knew how much getting a driver's license meant to her and how she wanted to help her in reaching her goal of being able to drive, Mary would have been facilitated to react much differently. If her mother had told her that there was no extra money to pay for driver's training, they could have collaborated about how to earn the necessary funds.

Planning about how to earn money for a driver's education course could have been a very bonding experience. Mary could have marketed herself as a babysitter. She could have gone door-to-door asking neighbors if they needed help with any household chores. She could have contacted others in her neighborhood and offered to weed part of their yard for a fee. Mary's mother could have budgeted $5.00 a week toward the price of the driver's education course and placed it in a jar so she and Mary could watch it grow. If possible, Mary and her mother could weed someone's yard together, or take in laundry. There are many creative ways to earn money.

Much of this dilemma could have been avoided altogether if Mary and her mother had planned for the day Mary could get a driver's permit and take driver's education classes. They would have had a much smoother path if this topic had been discussed before Mary was legally able to learn how to drive. If, for example, at age 14, Mary's mother had had a conversation with her about researching the costs involved with getting a driver's permit and license, they could have been working on this goal way before the time came. They could have been working on it together. Such an experience could have provided a fond lasting memory for each of them: how we worked together to get Mary a driver's license.

Driving Practice

As parents, one of the most important safety activities we can participate in is allowing our young adult to practice driving. This will necessitate taking time out of our schedules. It is an important negotiation with our teens because the more we can help them practice, the more competent they will be once they are on the road by themselves.

It may be tempting to enter this agreement with some trepidation. It can be anxiety evoking to be a passenger with a new driver behind the steering wheel. However, if a caregiver gives the impression that assisting their teen in the practice of driving is a burden and a chore, chances are that your young adult will not enjoy the experience either. We parents have the opportunity of giving our teens a memorable experience that they can share in years to come. Or, we can make these practice times a nagging, angry, demeaning experience for our teen—they will remember that too.

Driving Practice Contract

Agreements	My Responsibilities	Consequences for Breaking Agreements
Parents: Take teen to practice driving every Saturday morning at 9 A.M. for 45 minutes.	Parents: Make yourself available. Be at a designated meeting place (front door of your home) on time.	Parents: Teaching your teen that your word can't be trusted and that you don't respect this contract.
Teen: Rise promptly and meet your parent(s) at the designated meeting place at 9 A.M.	Teen: Get yourself up, dressed, fed, and on time at the door.	Teen: If late, even by one minute, no driving that Saturday.
Parents: Will not wake teen for driving practice.	Parents: Resist in taking on your teen's responsibility of getting up on time for their practice driving appointment (with you).	Parents: Teaching your teen that they don't have to be responsible for getting themselves up out of bed.
Teen: Agree to follow all driving laws during driving practice.	Teen: Learn the laws.	No practice for one week.
Parents: Take teen to a safe place for teen to practice driving.	Parents: Find a safe place for driving practice. If you select a busy thoroughfare or crowded parking lot, you may not blame teen for being anxious and scaring you with their driving.	Jeopardizing your teens and your own safety.

More About Car Contracts

It is crucial to have a Car Contract with your teen or young adult. This is an area in which financial and legal nightmares can happen. Without clear guidelines and a clear delineation of responsibilities for all parties involved, arguments, bickering, power struggles, resentments, and anger will occur. Why? Because your young adult will not know what is expected from them in order to have the privilege of driving, and he/she will "fight for fairness!" Having consequences for poor driving decisions come AFTER the event doesn't provide your young adult with the opportunity to choose between impulse and responsibility because they have not been given the outline for responsible behavior when behind the wheel.

Many guardians think, "Well, if my teen doesn't know how to act when driving, then they shouldn't be on the road." This is true! But physiologically, teens don't have a brain with a mature, developed capacity to differentiate negative consequences from impulsive decisions. So what parents think their young adult "should" know is often quite different from what a teen is actually mentally capable of considering.

Texting while driving is a topic that is consistently in the news. Many accidents have taken place because a driver was preoccupied communicating with someone on a cell phone. Driving while under the influence has resulted in innumerable deaths. Property damage, permanent physical impairments, and death have often been the result of a young adult's thrill-seeking by putting themselves in high-risk situations while behind the wheel. Even though a Car Contract won't prevent teens from entering dangerous situations, it will give a young adult pause to consider the consequences they are choosing by deciding to break any of the agreements.

Leave the guesswork out of teen driving. Leave "playing it by ear" on the curb. Provide your young adult with a contract so all parties will be clear on expectations and the consequences for deciding to not comply with prearranged agreements. That way, your young driver will be well equipped to decide to either keep their driving privileges, or to violate their agreements and choose the consequences by doing so.

In designing your Car Contract, be specific. Keep it short and simple. Don't become so detailed that your young adult has any room for confusion. Get a signature on this contract. No signature, no driving. That way, the parent has a bilateral agreement and their teen can't say, "You didn't tell me," or, "I didn't know."

On the following pages, you will find some sample Car Contracts. Adapt them to your personal needs.

Note that a Car Contract for driving is different from a contract regarding who pays for a car and driving expenses. Be specific. Usually more than one contract needs to be in place.

Driving Responsibilities

Justin

Justin was a very fun kid to have around. He cracked jokes, had lots of friends, was an average student, was on the football team, and had many females vying for his attention. Then Justin turned 16 and got his driver's license.

Justin's parents had always promised that if Justin "stayed out of trouble" (whatever that meant), when he was 16, they would buy him a car. And sure enough, Justin was a joy to have around. So on his 16th birthday, his mom and dad purchased a used red Mustang for him. Everyone was thrilled with the great deal Justin's parents were able to negotiate for the car. It was five years old, mechanically excellent, and had the additional bonus of a fabulous audio system. Justin was elated.

Mom and Dad turned the keys over to Justin after they added him and his car to their car insurance policy. The car insurance for a minor was substantial, but Justin's parents paid it without a contribution from their son. Then Justin got a speeding ticket. His parents paid it after having a "firm" conversation with him regarding responsible driving. After that, Justin got in a car accident. He rear-ended the car in front of him because "they slammed on the brakes and I didn't know they were going to do that." Justin's parents paid for the car repair for Justin's car and the other driver's car, so their insurance rates wouldn't go up. But the driver of the other car filed a claim for injury, so now Justin's parents had to involve their insurance carrier. Justin was encouraged to "be more careful," and he agreed to do so.

Finally, Justin received a DUI. He called his parents from the police department, and they immediately went to rescue him. Justin's dad hired "the meanest attorney I could find to get him off so it wouldn't be on his driving record." They paid $10,000 to their lawyer, and Justin received community service and a temporarily suspended license. Justin's mom then had to drive him to school.

This is a nightmare. If there had been a Car Contract in place, Justin would have known that all of his driving decisions would determine if he could continue to drive his red Mustang. Mom and Dad kept rescuing him from his bad judgment, so why would Justin, on his own, assume responsibility for his behavior?

Parents, save yourselves from this trauma. Make a Car Contract so that having the privilege to drive rests with your young adult.

This contract addresses driver responsibilities and the consequences for unsafe driving.

Driving Responsibilities Contract

Agreements	My Responsibilities	Consequences for Breaking Agreements
Teen: You will not drive under the influence of any intoxicating substance.	Teen: Call parents or sober relatives/friends for a ride home if you find yourself under the influence.	No car for three months. Parents: Will monitor for sobriety upon return home from an evening out. Teen: Take a drug test, if parents deem it necessary.
Teen: You are responsible for paying all tickets and possible legal fees for breaking the law.	Teen: Drive within the guidelines of the law.	Teen: Legal consequences, possible jail time, community service. Transportation to and from school or any other activity is the responsibility of teen.
Teen: Should you get a DUI, you are responsible for all legal fees and for getting to and from any required court appearances or court-mandated consequences.	Teen: Never risk your life or the lives of others by driving under the influence.	Teen: Having no parental support for getting you out of consequences due to your bad judgment.
Teen: There will be no engagement in high-risk car games.	Teen: Drive safely and follow the laws of the road. Cars are for transportation, not for games.	Teen: Engaging in high-risk car games indicates poor judgment. No car for three months.
Teen: No texting or cell phone use while driving.	Teen: Not to answer texts or calls while driving car. Pull over to the side of the road if it is necessary to communicate with someone.	Teen: The legal consequences for breaking any laws for texting or talking on cell phone while driving are yours.

I have read and understood this contract:

Signed: _____   Signed: _____

Date: _____   Date: _____

Purchase of a Car—Parents Pay

Parents must weigh how the gift of a car would affect their teen. Is your young adult really deserving of such a huge gift? What has your teen done to earn wheels? If you happen to have a young adult who has actually exhibited the ability to be responsible, then perhaps receiving a car would be a token of recognition. However, if you have a teen who has demonstrated that they have poor decision-making abilities, it might be wise for you to reconsider any inclination to give a car to your young adult.

This contract is not about car maintenance or who pays for what in relation to the teen driver. This contract is limited to the parameters around the purchase of a car as a "gift." Be sure to explain, in writing, to the recipient of the car that this IS a gift with strings attached. A Car Contract regarding driving responsibilities and a Car Contract regarding who pays for what, must be attached to and incorporated in the "gift" of a car to a teen/young adult.

Purchase of a Car: Parents Pay Contract

Agreements	My Responsibilities	Consequences for Breaking Agreements
Parents: Will purchase a car for young adult, not to exceed $10,000.	Parents: Research cars. Decide whether a new or used car is the best investment. Collaborate with teen regarding his/her options about type and color of car. Openly discuss the finances of the car. Set a top price. Don't pay more, or you will be teaching your teen that your limits are negotiable.	Parents: Far-reaching consequences for reneging on the promise of such a gift: Your teen will lose trust, respect, and security.
Parents: Pay for mechanic to evaluate car.	**Used Car** Teen: If car is not mechanically suitable, teen agrees to abide by the protective decisions of their parents without argument.	Teen: Delay of purchase of any car for one month.
Teen: Will be able to reject a car because of color or any other reason. Parents: Accept and respect teen's rejection of a car.	Teen: Advise your parents if there is a car color you won't consider.	Teen: Having parents find a car that is painted a color you hate.
Upgrades, if any, are at the expense of the teen. Permission must be granted by the parents.	Teen: If you want upgrades, research cost, save your money, and present your idea to your parents for approval or rejection. Teen to pay for upgrades.	Teen: Removal of any upgrade not approved by parents.
Teen: Stipulate transmission type.	Parents: Respect teen's preference.	Parents: Teen's resentments for not complying with this agreement.

Purchase of a Car—Split Costs

Working together with your teen to assist him/her in buying a car can provide a great opportunity to role-model about how one collaborates. There is no better way to teach your young adult about how to work with someone to reach a goal than doing it with a topic that captures their interest. Have you ever met a teen who isn't interested in driving or in having his/her own transportation? There are very few.

Knowing that your child will someday want a car, it might be advantageous to start planning with him/her when they are in their early teens. That way you can save together.

To collaborate means to work jointly with others in an endeavor. Before one enters this negotiation with one's offspring, all involved adults need to sit down and have a pre-discussion between themselves (without their teen present), regarding how much can be contributed toward the teen's car. Or if there is no ready cash available now, how can the car funds be saved for and earned? The adults must have an agreed-to plan in place BEFORE negotiating with their teen. That way, emotions are somewhat removed from the equation.

Now, if your teen is like many, he/she might try to guilt you when you announce that getting a car is going to be a joint financial responsibility. Spell it out: Adults and teen are going to have to contribute to the purchase of a car. Discuss how much money adults can contribute. Resist responding to statements like, "Gee, Jimmy's dad bought him a car," or, "How can I earn any money, I don't have a job?" Response to the first statement: "Jimmy is a lucky guy." PERIOD! No further discussion about this. The response to the second statement is: "Any ideas about how you could earn money?" And then be QUIET!!!!!! YOU don't have to provide the answer to this.

If your young adult is truly stumped about how to earn money or get a job, that is when parents can step in with supportive ideas. "Let's look online about jobs for kids under 18." There is a great deal of information. Examine sites such as snagajob.com. Sit with your teen and explore the information on the Web.

Another idea is to be a little entrepreneurial. Start when your child turns 13, and make it a big deal that your child and you get to work together to save for a car. Think about what businesses you can ALL start. Can you and your child get some gardening/weeding jobs? Is there a job for delivering newspapers in your area? What about grocery bagging at the local independent grocery store? Consider being a mother's aide and assisting with child care? There are a multitude of ideas that kids can come up with. How do you think your neighborhood lemonade stand started?

If parents can afford to do so, arrange for your younger teen to be able to earn small monetary rewards for homework turned in on time. This provides great incentive for being compliant with school demands. Ponder setting up rewards for any grade over a "C" on a test. This isn't about bribing your teen to get good grades; it's about crafting ways to make money for a car. Be creative. If parents set rewards too far in the future, like a certain grade point average at the end of the semester, it seems like eternity to a teen. Keep it concise. Keep it simple. Keep it short.

Purchase of a Car: Split Costs Contract

Agreements	My Responsibilities	Consequences for Breaking Agreements
Parents: Agree to contribute $5,000 toward the purchase of teen's car.	Parents: Have the funds available for use.	Parents: Breaking this agreement with their teen will have far-reaching consequences, including the teen's correct conclusion that his/her caregivers are not dependable or trustworthy.
Teen: Contribute at least $2,000 to the purchase of a car.	Teen: Save and earn the amount of money you will need to add to your parents' contribution to purchase a decent car. Minimum amount of your contribution is $2,000, payable once we start the car search.	Teen: With no saved car fund, no search for a car is started. No car.
Parents: Pay for diagnostic testing for the car.	Parents: Research the cost of diagnostic tests and have the money ready for one or two of them.	Parents: This is an opportunity to role-model "keeping one's word." If you don't come through, your teen will lose respect and deem you to not be a dependable person.
If teen is a minor, any car must be registered to parent. Teen and parent will split the cost. A side contract establishing percentage of ownership of the car will be made.	Teen: Research costs of registration for a car and give information to caregivers.	No car.
Parents: Gets to veto a car for mechanical reasons. Teen: Gets to veto a car for reasons of color, radio system, condition of tires, make and model, interior wear and tear.	Parents: Invest in a safe car for your teen. Teen: Have a car that you like that is within your price range.	Expectations set too high for the price teen and parents can pay will derail the enjoyment of buying a car. You are not going to get a Corvette that runs for $10,000.

Car Maintenance

So now you have purchased or helped purchase a car for your young adult. Now what? Who is going to pay for insurance, gas, tires, and oil? Have you even researched the cost of these items? Just the price of insurance for an underage driver can be staggering. If the financial responsibility for the upkeep of the car is not clearly delineated, there will be countless arguments about money for gas, money to replace the tires, etc.

Who is going to pay for repairs due to accidents? Does this depend on who was at fault? Who is going to determine who was at fault? Should there be a financial cap so parents aren't giving carte blanche to their teen regarding maintenance? Do not embark on the car gift/purchase until the details of who is going to pay for what have been ironed out.

As mentioned above, teenagers don't yet have the cognitive ability to look into the future and plan. The part of the brain that is in charge of this function is not well developed. Make sure you don't expect more from your young adult than he/she can deliver. If you, the caregiver, decide that your teen should have the privilege of driving a vehicle that is designated primarily for their use, then it is incumbent on you to present them with the whole package: car, maintenance, responsibilities, and obligations.

It is important to set your young adult up for success. Maintaining a car is a serious obligation. If your teen doesn't have a job, there is no way he/she can contribute to the maintenance of a vehicle. If guardians give the gift of a car and then expect a jobless teen to pay for upkeep, that is a formula for failure. It will lead to resentments, needless battles, stress, and frustration between the caregivers and the young adult.

If parents can't maintain a car for their teen, start to plan early to establish a savings account for the support and maintenance of a car. Thirteen-year-olds love to plan for the day when they can drive. Although the privilege of driving is a few years away (and to a 13-year-old this will seem like an eternity), young teens like to work on projects with their parents, especially projects like driving! Help them create ways to earn money. Help them establish savings goals and create rewards for reaching them. For example, when the first $100 has been deposited into their car maintenance savings account, take your teen to look at some cars that are for sale. That way, you are providing an education, and your teen can get some idea about what it would be like to have a car and be able to maintain it. When you are viewing a car that is for sale, ask about the costs of maintaining it. By occasionally looking at cars together, parents will be reinforcing the goal of being able to support and maintain a car.

For teens with a job, agreements about how much of their income will be spent/saved for the support of their car should be in writing so there is no confusion or misunderstandings.

Make these contracts to fit your situation. Included here are two different ideas.

Car Maintenance Contract: Parents Maintain Car

Agreements	My Responsibilities	Consequences for Breaking Agreements
Tires Parents: Will pay for new tires if indicated. Must have at least 30,000 miles on each set of tires. Tires that are needed before that will be expense of teen. There will be NO driving on unsafe tires. Tire rotation: Parents will pay for rotation of tires. Teen: Keep track of when tire rotation is needed and to remind parents.	Teen: Make sure enough air is in the tires, and that they are rotated on a regular basis. Parents: Write down mileage on car each time tires are replaced.	Teen: Pay for new tires if tires needed before 30,000 miles. No driving until you can save enough money to purchase four new tires. Parents: If you don't have record of car mileage when new set of tires are placed on car, you will have an expenditure of unnecessary funds for new ones.
Gas and Oil Teen: Teen will be reimbursed for gas and oil expenses or will ask for up-front money to pay for this maintenance. Parents: Reimburse teen within 3 days for gas when provided with a receipt.	Teen: Keep track of when an oil change is needed. Parents will not remind you. To give parents gas receipts. Parents: Provide funds to pay for oil change when requested by teen. Parents pay for gasoline for teen's car, up to $100/month.	Oil: Engine will be permanently damaged if not changed on a regular basis. If this happens, there will be no car, and no replacement car. Gasoline: No receipt for last gas purchase, , no reimbursement.
Interior Damage Teen: Teen will keep interior in the condition in which the car was purchased. Parents: Take detailed pictures of the car's interior when it is purchased.	Total responsibility of teen.	Teen: Will not drive the car until the interior damage has been repaired at teen's expense. Parents: Teaching your teen that (nonaccidental) damage to one's car's interior is not important.
Accidents Teen: Drive safely. Sometimes accidents just happen. Sometimes, the driver is at fault.	Teen: Police report must be filed. Police will determine fault. If they determine teen not at fault, parents will handle insurance claims, etc. If teen at fault, teen pays all expenses for repairs. Teen will pay the amount that is not covered if teen is found to have partial fault.	Teen: If accident is caused by you, consequence is driving around with a damaged car, or not having a car to drive due to irreparable damage.
Insurance Teen: If you are the cause of an increase in your car insurance premiums, you will pay the increase.	Parents: Pay for insurance for young adult's car.	Parents: Putting yourselves at risk financially for not insuring teen.

Signed: _____   Signed:_____

Date: _____   Date: _____

Car Maintenance: Shared Expenses

This can be a very tricky agreement because what happens when the parents have their part of the expenses and their young adult doesn't, or vice versa. There might be a temptation to front the money. DON'T! This will create yet another issue—when does one gets paid back for advancing car expenses?

Remember, this is a Car Maintenance Contract—not a borrower/lender agreement.

Car Maintenance Contract: Shared Expenses

Agreements	My Responsibilities	Consequences for Breaking Agreements
On the first of each month, teen will give parents half of the cost of the monthly insurance bill. Parents will make sure the bill is paid.	**Insurance** Teen: Deliver insurance funds by the first of each month to caregivers. Parents: Make sure the insurance bill is paid on time.	Lateness: Any late fees will be paid by the party who is late. If one party does not pay their half on time, no insurance will be paid that month. No one can drive the car until insurance is brought current. This often means starting over with a new insurance company, with one strike against you (failure to pay premium). This can be *very* expensive. Parent: Failure to pay insurance for one month can have financial ramifications. Call your insurance company for their policies regarding lack of payment for one or two months.
Parents: Pay half the cost of each oil change. Teen: Provide estimates and receipts for oil changes to parents.	**Oil Changes** Parents: Will pay half of the cost of each oil change. Teen: Present parents with oil change estimate from provider.	Permanent damage to car engine. No engine, no car, no driving.
Parents and Teen: Discuss and decide upon a monthly budget for gasoline.	**Gasoline** Parents: Will give $50/month gas card for gas purchases on the first of each month Teen: Responsible for any other gas purchases.	Teen: No gas to drive the car. Parents: If you decide not to respect this responsibility, teaching teen that contract is meaningless.
Teen: Drive safely. Sometimes accidents just happen. Sometimes, the driver is at fault.	**Accidents** Teen: Police report must be filed. Police will determine fault. If they determine teen not at fault, parents will handle insurance claims, etc. and pay for half of uncovered expenses. If teen at fault, teen pay all expenses for repairs. Teen will pay the amount that is not covered if teen is found to have partial fault.	Teen: If accident caused by you, consequence is driving around with a damaged car, or not having a car to drive due to irreparable damage. If you don't have a savings account for unexpected car maintenance, you might not be able to pay your half. Car will not be repaired until you have the required funds.
	Interior Damage Total responsibility of teen.	Driving a car with a damaged interior.

Signed: _____   Signed: _____

Date: _____   Date: _____

Sale of the Car Given as Gift by Parents

Parents Hold the Title

What do we do when all the rules have been broken and there is nothing left to do but to sell the car? Who gets the proceeds? Where are the proceeds placed? It is a gnarly issue because for parents to make the decision that their young adult is not responsible enough to drive and/or to have possession of a car, all the contracts have to have been violated by their teen. The decision to take wheels away from one's teenager will usually trigger a reaction of defiance, anger, tantrums, bargaining, begging, and evoke an "attitude from hell!" If we parents give in to this emotional manipulation, we are teaching our young adult that their acting out works! Our capitulation reinforces their bad behavior. Emotional manipulation techniques will go into the "OK Corral" (see Introduction), and we will have to live with them because they have been deemed acceptable by lack of intervention.

In the contract example below, we are assuming that there have been legal ramifications as a result of your teen's contract violations. This may not be the case. Personalize this contract to your needs and situation. Depending on your teen's situation, you may also want to create a contract about earning back driving privileges.

Car Sale Contract: Car as Gift by Parents

Agreements	My Responsibilities	Consequences for Breaking Agreements
Parents: Are selling the car they gave teen due to violation of previous contracts.	Parents: Advertise and find a buyer.	Parents: You will own an extra car that will give your teen hope that you will return it to him/her. Not selling the car neutralizes some of the effect of the seriousness of contract violations.
All proceeds from sale will be the parent's property.	Parents: Complete all paperwork required by the sale.	Owning an extra car.
Teen's driving privileges are revoked. As a minor, parents will not contribute to, or arrange for, teen to drive.	Teen: Not to drive.	Legal consequences will be the responsibility of teen. Any parent-paid court-ordered funds will be repaid from job and gifts of money on holidays and birthdays. A re-payment schedule will be created.
Parents: Will not provide transportation to school or court.	**Community Service** Teen: Get myself to and from community service locations.	Teen: Further consequences from the court for not meeting community service obligations.
Parents: Bail will not be posted if student gets arrested.	**Juvenile Hall/Jail** Teen: Your behavior has put you in this situation. It is your responsibility to learn your options. Parents: Will not bail teen out of juvenile hall or jail.	Parents: Teaching your young adult that they will be rescued by you so the consequences of poor judgment can be avoided.

Car Purchased Jointly by Teen and Parents: Title Held Jointly

Even though caregivers and their teen may have both financially contributed to the purchase of a car, when a minor is involved it is the parents who have legal responsibility. While minors can legally hold title to a car, usually a minor can't enter into a contract to buy one. So no matter who pays for the car, parents have control over if their teen has his/her name on the title. (Check the laws in your state.)

Make sure you cover who holds title in any Car Contract you create, even if you don't suspect that there is a possibility of having to withdraw car ownership/usage and driving privileges. If your teen's name is on the title, parents open themselves up to possible legal ramifications about transferring title.

If parents and their minor hold title jointly, the minor has to transfer title to the guardians in order for the parents to be able to pass along a clear title to a subsequent owner. As we can see, this could be a legally technical issue, so one might also want to contact legal aid or an attorney for advice.

Car Contract for Sale of the Car: Title Held Jointly

Agreements	My Responsibilities	Consequences for Breaking Agreements
If parents decide the car must be sold for violation of any previous Car Contract, teen agrees to sign over title to them.	Teen: Sign the necessary documents for the transfer of title. Parent: Provide the appropriate paperwork needed for title transfer.	Car won't be sold. Car won't be driven. Car will not be insured. The joint funds used to purchase car will be stuck in an asset of diminishing value. Parents: Can take teen to small claims court for not signing the title.
Proceeds from car sale to be put in a jointly held, two-signatures-required savings account at a bank of teen's choice.	Parent: Show teen the sale agreement so they are aware of the sale price. Parents will deposit the funds from sale into a bank account of teen's choice. Teen: Sign the appropriate bank documents to open the savings account.	Parent: Your teen has the ability to take you to small claims court should you not deposit the funds from the car sale into a joint bank account. Long-term trust issues.
Proceeds from car sale shall be split in the proportion each person gave to purchase the car. Teen: Will have no access to their funds until the age of 21, at which time your proportion of the proceeds in the account will be returned. Parents: After one week, parent may withdraw their proportion of the funds. Give teen an accounting. Have an acknowledgment signed.	Teen: Place your part of the proceeds in a joint savings account with parents. Savings account shall require two signatures for withdrawal.	Parents: Your teen has demonstrated poor judgment. If you return money from the car sale to them, chances are they will not use good judgment in spending it. Teen: Losing access to your part of the car investment.
	Advertising The costs to advertise car for sale will be deducted from teen's proceeds. Costs of marketing will be itemized.	Parents: Should not have to pay for teen breaking car agreements. Rescuing teen from this expense teaches teen that parents take on consequences that are not theirs to soften the outcome for their minor.
	Transfer Fees Will be deducted from teen's proceeds of sale.	Parents: Should not have to pay for teen breaking car agreements. Rescuing teen from this expense teaches teen that parents take on consequences that are not theirs to soften the outcome for their minor.

Earning Back Driving Privileges

When we take away something from our young adults, it is ALWAYS important to provide them with a way to earn back privileges. If your teen has broken all his/her Car Contracts, YOU have to decide whether it is worth the risk of returning driving privileges. We don't have to think of this as an "all or nothing" proposition. Perhaps half-measures will avail us some mutual goodwill.

What if you were able to monitor the entire driving experience by allowing your teen to drive your car with you in it? Yes, we know that this might sound like a consequence for YOU, but if this is the carrot that will put our teen back on the right track, why not? Initially, your teen might think this is a "stupid," "weird," or "certifiable" idea, and if this is what happens when you propose it, so be it. Take "NO!!!!" for an answer, and don't mention the idea again. However, one thing we know about most young adults is that they LOVE to drive! So even if you are in the car, for some teens, driving with YOU is better than not driving at all.

Consider providing a way for your young adult to earn back driving privileges. Think about what steps you want your teen to take to earn them. Grades? Completing chores around the house without a reminder? Turning in homework on time for one week? How would driving you to and from the grocery store be? Or, driving you to and from a medical appointment? When a young adult has totally failed in the "show me you are responsible" arena, sometimes providing a way to earn back self-respect is vital.

Earning Back Driving Privileges Contract

Agreements	My Responsibilities	Consequences for Breaking Agreements
Due to violation of all Car Contracts, teen has had driving privileges suspended for a period of two months. Teen: To enter the path of earning back driving privileges, I will not drive any vehicle.	Teen: Do not drive any vehicle no matter what the circumstances. Parent: Do not make any exceptions to this agreement.	Teen: Legal consequences. Eliminating any further way to earn back driving privileges.
After two months of no driving, teen may earn back the ability to drive parent to and from requested destinations.	Teen: On a week-to-week basis, (beginning on a Monday, and ending on a Friday) provide written proof from all teachers that daily homework has been turned in on time.	No teacher notes, no driving.
While driving, teen to obey all driving laws.	Teen: Abide by speed limits and other driving parameters.	Violation of driving laws = no driving.
After two months of abiding by this contract, open discussion about driving the family car without a caregiver riding along.	Teen: Follow this contract to the letter. No exceptions.	Not driving by oneself.
If driving privileges are earned back, a new Car Contract will be created.	Teen: Participate in negotiating a new Car Contract.	No return of driving privileges.

What a Choice: A Car or a Bike!

Siblings Sharing a Car

Susan and Greg

Greg was Susan's older brother. He was 17 and Susan was 16 when they were given a car—to share—by their parents. At first they were ecstatic! Their own wheels! WOW! Greg pictured taking girls out on dates and driving himself to football practice. Susan thought it would be so kewl to drive her friends to and from school with a stop at the local fast-food hangout on the way home. Greg and Susan's parents experienced some relief because they wouldn't have to chauffeur their kids back and forth to school, sporting events, team practices, and other extracurricular activities. Their mom also dreamed of sending one of them grocery shopping or running other errands for her. Everyone had a different expectation about how the car was going to be utilized. There was not a discussion about who got to use the car when, and for what purposes.

Friday came. Greg had a date. Susan had made plans with her girlfriends that she would pick them up to go to a movie. Greg's mom wanted him to pick her up at her job because Greg's dad had to use their car for work. Greg and Susan hadn't checked out their plans with each other. Greg picked up his mother. When they returned home from their day, Greg parked the car to go in the house to eat and get ready for his date. He and Susan passed each other as Susan was leaving the house to go get her pals.

Greg said, "Where are YOU going?" Susan replied, "To pick up Jackie and Betsy to go out to eat and to the movies." Greg said, "Oh no, YOU aren't! I'm using the car for a date!" And then it got nasty!!

Immediately Greg and Susan involved their mother to solve their problem. How can one actually be fair in a situation like this? This was really no one's fault. They just hadn't checked with each other on who was planning to use the car. Now Mom is in a position of creating a win/lose situation with her kids. No matter what she decides, one of her teens will think she's not being fair and favoring the other sibling. This is a lose-lose for mom.

After a huge blowup between Susan and Greg and their mother, Mom decided that Greg could use the car for his date, and when her husband returned home, she would pick up Susan's friends and drive them to and from the movie. Susan accused her mom of favoring Greg and ruining her evening. In an effort to show her mother how hurt she was, Susan called her friends and canceled their plans. And all of this could have been avoided!

After this episode, Susan and Greg's mom and dad decided that a contract about driving privileges would help preclude any future issues. They involved their teens in the creation of the contract so it became a joint effort. Everyone had a voice. One thing about a contract is that it can be an evolving document that sustains change when new situations arise.

Susan and Greg's Car Contract made it clear who could use the car and when. It delineated responsibilities. It created a line of communication between siblings. It also introduced a reason for Susan and Greg to develop negotiating skills. Having a contract creates more opportunities for those win/win situations.

If there was ever a topic that was the source of sibling arguments, sharing a car hits the top of the list. Sharing a car provides so very many opportunities for misunderstandings, manipulation, power struggles, and power plays. It also enables brothers and sisters to hone their negotiating skills. This is why it is critical that there be a contract in place. It would be beneficial to have those parties who are sharing a car to be a part of the creation of this contract. That way, they feel they have had a voice in the "sharing car" structure.

Siblings Sharing a Car Contract

Agreements	My Responsibilities	Consequences for Breaking Agreements
Greg uses the car Monday, Wednesday, and Friday. Susan uses the car Tuesday, Thursday, Saturday.	Schedule things I need to drive to on those days.	If Greg schedules an event on the days he doesn't have the car, he either won't make his appointment or he'll have to reschedule or find other transportation. If Susan schedules an event on the days she doesn't have the car, she either won't make her appointment, or she'll have to reschedule transportation.
Last Driver: Leave the car clean each time you finish driving it.	**Cleanliness** Each party is to leave the car clean for the other. That includes but is not limited to debris, food containers, papers, clothes. Parties will rotate washing the car inside and out, on the first Saturday of each month.	If car is delivered with debris in it, loss of driving privilege the next time you are scheduled. If car is not washed once a month on a rotating basis, loss of car privilege at the end of the month, on a weekend day.
Changes to this schedule must be in writing, signed by both parties, witnessed by one parent. Dates must be specified on each schedule change. Limit of one schedule change per person per week.	**Bartering for Schedule Changes** Make sure there is a date on any schedule change. Be sure one parent signs the schedule change. The person who is requesting the schedule change is responsible for putting the agreement in writing, putting on the date, and procuring one parent's signature.	No date on schedule change, the change will not be honored. Any arguing about the schedule change prior to a signed contract, the schedule change will not be honored. Failure to meet ALL the requirements listed in the adjacent box will result in no schedule change.
Money or favors will NEVER be the currency with which one barters for schedule change. Schedule change involves trading one day for another.	Abide by the terms of schedule change in this contract.	Violation of this agreement will result in not using the car for one week.
Parents: Procure two credit cards from two different companies so there will be no argument about charges. Teen: Provide parents with gas receipts and fill the gas tank when it is ½ empty.	**Gasoline** Parents will give each party to this contract a gas credit card. Receipts for gasoline will be given to Mom or Dad. Credit card to be used only for gasoline unless otherwise agreed upon. When the gas tank reaches ½ empty, the party driving the car at that time is to fill up the gas tank. Each driver to check the amount of gas in the car before returning it home from use.	Charging other items on gas credit card will result in loss of car privileges for one week. Returning car home from use with the tank ½ or less full will result in suspension from the car for one week.

Siblings Sharing a Car With Parents

Parents: here you are with two teens that both have driver's licenses! And YOU have ONE car! Everyone needs it! This is a situation that can cause tension not only between siblings, but between parents, and between parents and their young adults. Charges of "You're not fair" or "You favor Susan more" can be levied. If you are like most parents, these accusations can elicit feelings of guilt and angst about exactly HOW to be fair.

Having a contract will save you hours of negotiating, explaining, and bargaining time. It will rescue you from the sibling debates about who said they needed the car on what day. Remember, this is YOUR car, and you are LOANING it to your teen. There is no entitlement here. It is by your good graces that you are sharing your car.

Bob and Katy

Bob is 17 and Katy, his sister, is 16. Katy just got her driver's license, and she is very excited about the prospects of driving herself to school, to after-school activities, and to visit her friends. Bob has been "sharing" his parent's car with them. He has been able to drive to his activities, run errands for his parents, and has been happy with the car arrangements. Now his little sister has her license and he has to split his car privileges with her. Bob has some resentment about this.

Katy is planning to hang out with her girlfriends after school on Friday. She made plans with them to go to the mall and get something to eat. It will be her first outing with her friends with Katy as the driver. Bob, who has had the car every Friday, made plans to work out at the gym with some of his buddies after school, like he usually does. Each one of them, in their mind, has reserved the car, but neither of them has discussed their plans with each other.

Come breakfast on Friday morning, they each discover that the other has plans for the car, and on top of that, their dad thought he had told Bob that he needed the car that day for a last-minute business meeting he had to attend. Can you imagine the uproar that ensued? Dad stormed out of the house and drove away. Bob and Katy were left to figure out how to get to school. Their after-school plans were ruined. Everyone was angry with each other.

Such occurrences can be so easily prevented by having a written contract about who gets the car and when. This contract can be negotiated at the beginning of each month. It requires planning on the part of the teens, and what a great way to help your young adult acquire some organization skills! It requires flexibility on the part of all parties because unexpected things come up, like business appointments in the example above. It requires collaboration and communication, which are two extremely important skills to have in interpersonal relationships, work arenas, and childrearing. While sharing your car with your young adults can be an inconvenience, just think about the learning opportunities you are giving them!

Siblings Sharing a Car With Parents Contract

Agreements	My Responsibilities	Consequences for Breaking Agreements
Parents: Parental needs for our car supersede the needs of any other driver.	Parents and Teens: Schedule times for use.	Parents: If you don't involve yourself with the car scheduling, you invite chaos, arguments, and lack of respect for this contract by teens.
Parents: Will work out a schedule with teens that will attempt to satisfy their driving needs. This will be in the form of a calendar that will be posted on the refrigerator.	Parents: Have a family meeting about driving to determine set times when teens can use car. See example of calendar, below.	Parents: Chaos from having to decide on the spur of the moment who can drive the car. Having to mentally keep track of who gets to drive, when, where, why, with fairness in mind. Teens: Rightly accusing parents of "not being fair."
Teen: Check amount of gas in car before driving it. Take photo of it with your phone, or have your parent validate how much gas there is.	**Gasoline** Parents: Will give teen the use of a credit card to be used ONLY for gas. It is teen's responsibility to check the amount of gas in car before using it. Teen: Will give parent receipt after each fill-up.	Parents: Might have to pay for car towing if car runs out of gas. Teen: If you don't check amount of gas in car before using it and you don't ask for a credit card, YOU will be responsible for any costs connected to getting fuel.
Teen: The privilege of driving this car requires that you keep it clean. Any debris left in the car including homework, books, shoes, etc., will be either thrown away or kept in a baggie for one week. Parents: Even though you own this car, it is your responsibility to keep it clean for the next user.	**Cleanliness** Teens and Parents: Keep the car free of articles and garbage. Take pictures of the condition of the car before you drive it if it is delivered to you in an unclean condition.	Teens: Loss of car for one scheduled day. Parents: If you deem yourself exempt from this agreement, you are teaching your teens that they don't have to honor it either. Effectively makes agreement null and void ... parent's choice.
Teens and Parents: May trade designated days of use.	**Trading Designated Days of Use** Teen: Negotiate trades at least two days before needed. Trades are to be written with signature by each party, witnessed by one parent. If one party is not able to trade, the other party has to make other arrangements.	Teen: Arguing about trades results in the loss of one scheduled driving privilege for all parties involved in the argument.

Sharing Car Calendar Example

Sunday	Monday	Tuesday	Wednesday	Thursday	Friday	Saturday
	1 Mom has car all day	2 Susan has car for swim practice from 3:30–6:00 Greg has car for Scouts from 6:00–9:00	3 Dad has car all day.	4 Mom has car all day.	5 Greg has car all day if he meets criteria of the Car Contract.	6 Susan has car all day if she meets criteria of the Car Contract.
7 Mom and Dad have car all day.	8 Mom has car all day.	9 Susan has car for swim practice from 3:30–6:00. Greg has car for Scouts from 6:00–9:00.	10 Dad has car all day.	11 Mom has car all day.	12 Susan has car all day if she meets criteria set forth in the Car Contract.	13 Greg has car all day if he meets criteria set forth in the Car Contract.
14 Susan has car from 1:00–6:00 for activities with friends.	15 Mom has car all day.	16 Susan has car for swim practice: 3:30–6:00. Greg has car for Scouts from 6:00–9:00.	17 Dad has car all day.	18 Mom has car all day.	19 Greg has car all day if he meets criteria set forth in the Car Contract.	20 Susan has car from 9:00–3:00. Mom and Dad have car from 3:00 on.
21 Mom and Dad have car all day.	22 Mom has car all day.	23 Susan has car for swim practice: 3:30–6:00. Greg has car for Scouts from 6:00–9:00.	24 Dad has car all day.	25 Mom has car all day.	26 Mom has car all day.	27 Dad has car until 5:00. Greg has car from 5:00 to midnight curfew.
28 Susan has car all day.	29 Mom has car all day.	30 Susan has car for swim practice: 3:30–6:00. Greg has car for Scouts from 6:00–9:00.		And so on!		

Car Contracts: Other Things to Consider

1. Parents pay for car and all expenses. Driver has to have a certain grade point average a semester BEFORE any car is provided. Driver has to maintain that GPA for continued access to the car.

2. Running errands: Consider reimbursing driver for gas. It is a way to show you value his/her time.

3. Teen must find/keep a job to support the car.

4. Put the amount of the cost of car insurance clearly in the contract. The amount of the monthly insurance is _____, which is due and payable at the first of every month. This amount of money will be delivered to _____, in cash. This can be on a separate page attached to the contract.

5. Teen and parents will save $500 each and deposit it in a joint savings account as a nest egg for car repairs. Two signatures will be required to use this account.

6. Upgrades: no upgrades to any part of the car without caregivers' permission. Upgrades are the total expense of the young adult and must be paid for in cash. Where funds are coming from must be shown to caregivers.

7. When purchasing or considering the purchase of a car, parents are to accompany teen to any inspection to be sure there are no mechanical problems.

8. If agreements are broken, give your teen a way to earn back privileges. Make it a short duration of time. For example: Your 10-year-old reports that her brother, who was driving her to swim class, was texting while driving. The consequence in the contract could be no use of the car for one week, or taking the cell phone away for one week.

9. Seat belts for the driver, and for all passengers, need to be buckled at all times. If you think you need this as part of your contract, add it.

10. When will you allow your teen to practice driving? They have to practice! Maybe incorporate it in your Car Contract.

There may be other ideas that come up for you. Be creative. Just keep contracts short, precise, and understandable.

CHAPTER 9

Going to College

Deciding What College to Attend

Much of the time, it can be confusing and scary for a 17- or 18-year-old to figure out how to approach finding out about colleges, apply for admission, figure out transportation to and from, or make decisions about all that is required to be a college student. You may have a straight-A++ student who wants to attend the most expensive university in the country, but without a scholarship or getting a student loan, there might be no possible way for your young adult to attend that particular college. Every parent wants their teen's college experience to be a memorable one. Don't set your young adult up for disappointments.

Discuss with your teen where he/she wants to go to college.

Listen to their reasoning.

Listen to their ideas about how much it will cost and where they are thinking they will get the funds to attend the college of their choice.

It doesn't matter if their thoughts don't make sense to you and are riddled with idealism and denial… YOU need to listen to them.

Discuss with your teen the pros and cons of each college under consideration. Make a list of the pros and cons, so you won't forget what was discussed.

Make a budget. Tell your teen what you can afford to contribute toward their college education.

If the family cannot pay for all the college expenses, then discuss with your teen possible financing options: scholarships, student loans, borrowing from a trust fund, etc.

Most 18-year-olds don't know how to apply for a scholarship or student loan. YOU get to educate yourself and help them.

Once you have determined a budget, make a list of the top five affordable colleges. As number six, throw in one college that doesn't meet budget criteria and, just for the fun of it, apply for a scholarship at that college … one never knows what just might happen.

Take your teen to visit the top five colleges on the list.

Listen to your teen's feedback about the colleges. Remember, YOU are not the one selecting the college.

Assist your young adult in the application process. Assist your teen in the scholarship application process. When visiting your colleges set up meetings with the student loan department. Attend that meeting with your teen.

Don't miss this chance to bond with your teen. They will never forget how supportive and helpful you were during this process. Create treasured memories for them. They will most likely pass this on to your grandchildren. Think of the lovely legacy that you, the parents, have an opportunity to pass on.

The College Contract

You now have a child who has earned the privilege to go to college. Under what conditions will you provide spending money, tuition, room and board for your college student? He/she needs to know, so the consequences for not following through with their educational responsibilities will be known BEFORE any information reaches you regarding their college attendance or performance that could influence you to change your financial support.

Below are some ideas for agreements that can be made regarding the privilege of attending college. Add or delete as necessary.

Parents will pay for tuition, room and board, books, and academic supplies.

A spending allowance of $_____ per month will be deposited in your bank account on the first of every month. This will cover incidentals. No other cash contributions will be made during the rest of the month.

Student may have his/her car at college. Use of the car will fall under the Car Contract.

For the privilege of complete financial support, student will maintain a grade point average of 3.0 (B) (parents decide).

Student to sign any documents necessary to allow parents access to his/her academic records. Student to provide parents with a copy of that signed release document.

At the end of every grading period, grades to be sent to parents direct from the college.

College Contract: Parents Pay All Expenses

Agreements	My Responsibilities	Consequences for Breaking Agreements
Tuition, room and board, books, and academic supplies paid by parents.	A consistent GPA of 3.0 (parent decides what is acceptable).	<u>Parents</u>: Will stop paying college expenses. To earn these back, student will pay all expenses until a semester/quarter showing a 3.0 GPA is produced, at which time parental support will be reestablished.
A joint bank account will be established. On the first of every month parents will deposit $500.00 for incidentals.	Do not exceed spending my monthly allowance so as to avoid overdrafts.	<u>Parents</u>: Failure to deposit monthly allowance on time will result in a $5.00 fine for every day the deposit is late. Those additional funds will be deposited into student account. <u>Student</u>: Any overdrafts will be deducted from student's allowance. (See below for further comments about this.)
	Car See Car Contract.	
<u>Teen</u>: Advise parents at least one month in advance of the dates they will need to leave and return. <u>Parents</u>: Make necessary reservations or reimburse cost of gas for the drive home.	**Transportation Home** <u>Parents</u>: Responsibility to make arrangements with student regarding holiday plans or other occasions for coming home. Parents will pay for any flights or other transportation home. If a car is the mode of transportation home, when presented with a receipt for gas, parents will reimburse student that amount. <u>Teen</u>: Notify your parents of your vacation schedule within 1 month of the vacation.	<u>Teen</u>: If you don't advise your parents about your vacation dates at least one month in advance, they will not be responsible for making your travel reservations or for transportation from airports/bus stations/train depots. You will pay for any increase costs caused by you not providing your parents with the necessary information to make reservations 30 days in advance. <u>Parents</u>: You will be teaching your teen that they don't need to give you notice about their plans and that they don't need to consider or respect your schedule.
<u>Teen</u>: Stay within your monthly financial allotment.	**Credit Cards** Alternative to the monthly cash deposit—see Further Considerations, below.	Overages will result in the loss of the credit card.

The College Contract: Further Considerations

Overdrafts: Having an overdraft is a total waste of money. A double consequence is agreed to here: The student will pay the overdraft. The amount of the overdraft will be deducted from the student's monthly allowance. In essence, the student pays twice. This provides real incentive not to overdraw one's bank account.

Late deposits: The consequences for not depositing the monthly allowance on time are the parents'. This benefits the student. Parents will be fined $5.00 for each day the student's deposit is late, and that amount will be added to the deposit made to the student.

Failure to keep the designated GPA: If student decides to not keep a 3.0 GPA (or whatever GPA is determined), then all financial assistance will be terminated. To earn the reinstatement of parental financial support, student will remain in college at his/her own expense. Upon the receipt of documentation from the college that a 3.0 GPA has been earned, parental financial support will be reinstated.

Credit cards: If a credit card is to be used for the $500.00/month student allowance (instead of cash), then further agreements are necessary. Ask your bank to limit the monthly amount charged on the credit card to $500.00. Or, instead of a credit card, provide a debit card. You can also have a credit card that has a maximum of $500.00 credit.

Whatever you decide is your best way of providing a student allowance, there must be a consequence for overspending. The best and most meaningful consequence is usually loss of the privilege for a certain number of days/months. Provisions must be made as to how the student can earn the privilege back.

Having Your Car at College Contract

Agreements	My Responsibilities	Consequences for Breaking Agreements
All agreements of the Car Contract are incorporated in this agreement.	Abide by the agreements of the Car Contract.	Loss of car at college.
No other party shall drive the car. No more than three other people in the car at a time.	You are the only one who drives the car. Do not overcrowd the car.	Huge insurance liabilities for parents and driver. Loss of car and of all car privileges at college and at home.
Car shall not be driven on extended trips without parents' permission.	Get permission from parents before leaving the city in which the college is located.	Loss of use of the car for one college quarter/semester.
Teen is responsible for oil changes and gasoline expenses to be paid out of the monthly allowance.	Give receipts to parents. Keep the car in mechanically good condition.	Any mechanical problems with the car that arise as a result of not maintaining it become the expense of the teen.
Teen will immediately pay any ticket that is issued because of violating any law.	Pay any parking or speeding tickets. Inform my guardians.	Loss of using car while at college.

Having a car at college is a huge privilege. Be sure you attach any Car Contracts to this contract so that the responsibilities of each party are completely clear.

If your teen has a job, college fund, or inheritance, it is important to have financial agreements about how much they will contribute toward their college education. Tailor-make each contract to your needs. Below are a few examples. Paying all one's college expenses when you are a young adult is a huge responsibility. The aspiration alone demands respect. The teenage brain is not quite matured enough to do concrete future planning, so gentle guidance from one's parents might be needed and appreciated.

Teen and Parents Share College Expenses: Teen With a Job Contract

Agreements	My Responsibilities	Consequences for Breaking Agreements
Teen's job at college pays $1,000 per month.	Keep your job or find another that pays equal or more before leaving the job you have.	No money to live on.
Teen: Is to contribute $400 per month toward room and board in the dorms. That money is to be given to the dorm on the first of each month.	Make sure that your share of room and board is paid by the first of each month. Get a receipt and send your parents a copy.	Losing your ability to live in the dorm.
Parents: Will pay the balance of the room and board expenses.	Parents: Send a check to the dorm by the first of each month, and send teen a copy of the canceled check or receipt.	Making getting a college education more difficult for teen. Teen losing trust in parents.
Parents: Will assist teen with applying for a student loan to cover tuition and books.	Parents: Complete your part of the student loan application in a timely manner. Teen: Make and attend an appointment at the student loan center to get paperwork for parents and self, and follow through in delivering it to parents.	Not attending college due to lack of ability to pay tuition and books.
Parents: Will provide transportation for young adult to and from college for beginning of school year, Thanksgiving, Christmas/Chanukah, Easter/Passover (if applicable).	Teen: Provide parents with dates of your holiday availability at least one month before the event. Parents: Arrange departures and arrivals through planning with teen.	If transportation other than one's car is needed to fulfill this agreement, and if teen has not made arrangements with parents at least one month before the event, teen will have to pay the difference between the cost of holiday travel fares and regular fares.

College Expenses Contract: Teen Pays All

Agreements	My Responsibilities	Consequences for Breaking Agreements
Student will get a student loan to cover tuition and books.	Make an appointment with a financial aid counselor.	No student loan, no college.
Caregivers: Will complete the necessary paperwork for financial aid within one week of receiving it.	Complete financial aid paperwork in a timely manner so your young adult can attend college.	Poor role modeling for your teen. Teaching teen YOU are not responsible or supportive. Unknown long-term consequences.
Teen: May continue to live at home with all meals provided at parent's expense.	Teen: Abide by the Living at Home While Attending College Contract. Parents: Provide teen with a place to sleep and study, and provide him/her with nutritious food to eat.	Teen: Not living at home and having to provide for my own room and board.
Extra money from student loan will be put in a bank account requiring two signatures and be used only for expenses pertaining to school. Financial aid money is to be used ONLY for the expenses related to being a student!	Teen: To request assistance from parents about how to determine if there are extra funds from your student loan. Once done, open a joint banking account, make a monthly budget and keep to it.	If teen doesn't have a job, and "decides to spend extra financial aid money on superfluous items, teen is choosing not to have money for living/school expenses, and parents will not sign any further student loan applications.
	Extras Any extra expenses for school, cell phone, social events, are the responsibility of the student.	Not saving for extras will mean you won't have things like your yearbook, etc.

Relative Pays for College Expenses

When Grandma and Grandpa offer to pay a young adult's college expenses, they are providing their grandchild with opportunities that will affect their lives in a positive way. There is no greater gift than the gift of an education. What a generous offer! What a lovely gift! Or is it a gift? Do Grandma and Grandpa expect to get repaid? How should they distribute the funds? Are expectations attached to their gift?

It is crucial to have agreements with Grandma and Grandpa or other relatives who are contributing, so there will be no misunderstandings. Do Grandma and Grandpa want to see grades? What kind of involvement do they want in their grandchild's choice of major, classes, etc.? Clear these things up *before* accepting any financial assistance from relatives. When having more than one relative contribute to a relative's college education, make a contract with each one, so ALL parties know what the agreements and responsibilities are. This will diminish the possibility for misunderstandings.

BEFORE you make your offer to fund your relative's college education, make sure you become informed about all the tax benefits and/or consequences. Check with your accountant regarding how much money one can gift per year. How does this affect you and your recipient's taxes? Check about the tax benefits of opening an education fund. Get all the advice you can from financial planners and your tax advisor. This way, one never has to retract an offer to fund a college education due to ignorance.

BEFORE you make an offer to fund your relative's college education, put a ceiling on the amount of money you have in mind. If you are planning on receiving a tax benefit from making a gift, find out about the annual limits on this.

BEFORE you make an offer to fund your relative's college education, or BEFORE you decide to accept any such offer, decide what, if anything, is wanted in return. Write it out. Is it asking too much? Chris, a past client, came to therapy because his aunt and uncle had offered to pay his college tuition, room, board, and books for four years, in return for a promise to care for them when they could no longer care for themselves. Chris thought this was a great offer, but one he was not willing to accept because of the long-term, open-ended strings attached to it. He had a very difficult time explaining to them why he couldn't accept their generous offer. They had never had children of their own and viewed Chris like a son. Needless to say, they were highly insulted when Chris had to decline their offer. Was it an offer, or was it a manipulation? We each have to decide for ourselves. What might look fantastic and generous at the outset might turn out to have unacceptable terms.

When accepting the gift of a college education, set up some accountability for the recipient. Having the college mail semester grades, and establishing a grade point average that must be sustained for continued support is usually the most effective.

Relative Pays for College Expenses Contract

Agreements	My Responsibilities	Consequences for Breaking Agreements
Grandma and Grandpa are paying tuition, room and board for the first year of college. According to the college, this contribution will be $_____ per year, or $_____ per semester. Checks will be sent directly to the college at least one week before due date. The amount of this contribution is not to exceed $13,500 per year.	Teen and parents: Present any bills regarding tuition, room and board to Grandma and Grandpa within the week that they are received from the college. Provide grandparents with stamped envelopes addressed to the college. Grandparents: Pay these bills on time, and let your grandchild know when you sent your check to the college.	Not having your tuition, room and board paid. Grandparents: Loss of trust and respect from your grandchild and your grandchild's parents.
Parents: Are paying for required books and study materials. Semester budget is $300. Any funds requested above this amount will require an itemized list of costs per book and other needed materials.	Teen: If more than $300 per semester is required so all assigned books can be purchased, an itemized list with prices/book will be presented to parents in order to receive extra funds.	Not being able to have all the books you need for your classes.
End of semester grades are to be sent to parents and grandparents directly from the college. Teen will sign a Release of Information form (ROI) so college can comply with this agreement. Teen to provide his grandparents and parents with a copy of the ROI within one week from registering for classes.	Teen: After the first semester, if grades aren't provided to grandparents and parents by the college, tuition will not be paid for the subsequent semester. If a copy of the ROI you signed is not given to your parents and grandparents, no tuition paid for the subsequent semester.	Having to get a loan for, or earn your own college tuition, room and board.
A GPA (grade point average) of _____ must be sustained each semester for grandparents to continue paying for room and board and tuition.	Teen: Sustain the expected GPA.	Forfeiting grandparents paying room and board and tuition until a GPA of _____ is achieved.
Tuition increases will be presented to grandparents for their decision about how to proceed.	Teen and parents: Keep grandparents advised about increases in tuition, room and board. To accept whatever grandparents decide about covering college increases.	If grandparents aren't advised about increases, those will have to be covered through another source or not at all, which will mean college tuition, room and board will not be paid in full. Any portion of increases that are paid due to lack of informing grandparents will be the responsibility of the teen and parents to cover.

Flunking Out of College

Michael

Michael was a good student in high school. He was accepted to the college he wanted to attend, pledged a fraternity, and because there was no College Contract regarding expectations and consequences for poor performance, Michael had a fabulous year… of being at every party thrown on Greek Row. He rarely attended classes. After his first semester, he was put on academic probation. At the end of his second semester, he received a letter from the college saying he couldn't return for at least a semester due to not maintaining the minimum academic requirements to remain in school. Michael's parents were devastated. Because Michael didn't actually believe that there would be enforced consequences for his 1.5 GPA, he was shocked when he received his expulsion letter.

In June, Michael, and all the belongings from his dorm room, arrived on his parent's front porch. Michael's mom had turned his bedroom into the art room she had always wanted. She had hired a carpenter to custom build special shelving. Mom did NOT want to give up her art room.

Dad had cleaned the garage that had been a mess for years. Michael loved to begin woodworking projects. The entire family agreed that he had a talent for making things out of wood. The problem was that he rarely finished them, but when he did, the end product was spectacular. Dad discovered he liked his immaculate garage that was free of clutter. Dad didn't want anyone messing up his garage again.

Michael's sister, Anna, 15 years of age, was also a painter, and she and her mom enjoyed painting together in the new art room. They would listen to Anna's music and then alternate to Mom's music while they painted. They had discussed taking up sculpturing and how the new art room might accommodate the needed equipment.

But here was 19-year-old Michael on the doorstep, with no plans, no bed, no great "welcome home, son," and no immediate prospects for a job. He had told his family that he was "doing really well" in school, so the expulsion came as a total surprise to his parents. Michael's family seemed unwelcoming, and this led Michael to assume that his parents and sister didn't really love him, or want him around.

Michael and his family would have been better prepared for his return home if there had been an agreement about what would happen should Michael not honor his college responsibilities. While Michael felt unloved, his parents and sister thought there was something different about Michael. He appeared detached, unconnected, lazy, unmotivated. They suspected he was smoking pot. They were greatly concerned. They were also angry. What happened to their dream of summer and holiday visits, college graduation, helping to find that first apartment, celebrating that first good paying job, etc.?

Having your college student flunk out of school needn't be that shock that totally blindsides an entire family. Before your teen leaves for college, have a "Being Expelled From College Contract" in place. Don't delude yourself by thinking, "Oh, this can never happen to me."

Being Expelled From College

If parents have a College Contract in place, wherein grades are delivered to them at the end of each quarter or semester, the need for this type of contract shouldn't arise. However, anyone can be expelled from college for certain types of abhorrent behavior, so having this contract affixed to the College Contract could be a prudent thing to do. While this contract might seem a little strict and harsh, this is only a skeleton from which you can design your own contract. Remember, your teen CHOSE his/her predicament by consciously electing not to keep up the required GPA. Hopefully, these serious consequences for wasting the opportunity to attend college will deter your teen from being lax about academic diligence.

If teen is expelled from college for any reason, the following will take place:

Being Expelled From College Contract

Agreements	My Responsibilities	Consequences for Breaking Agreements
<u>Teen</u>: Will have _____ weeks to find a job. Teen will pay $_____ per month to caregivers for room and board.	<u>Teen</u>: Procure employment.	No job within the allotted time limit will result in being handed a 30-day notice to vacate the family home and support yourself.
The Living at Home With a Job Contract is affixed and incorporated into this contract.	<u>Teen</u>: To comply with and respect the terms of the Living at Home With a Job Contract.	See Living at Home With a Job Contract.
<u>Teen</u>: May live at home for a period of one year before having to move into a place of his/her own.	<u>Teen</u>: After living at home for 10 months, teen to locate an affordable living arrangement and to prepare to move.	Being homeless.
<u>Teen</u>: May elect to attend a local college in addition to having a job. Parents will not contribute to financing this choice other than to provide room and board. If teen achieves a GPA of _____ per semester, the original college financing agreement will fall back into place. Teen has also then earned the privilege of living at home until an AA degree is earned and they transfer to a four-year college.	<u>Teen</u>: Decide the pros and cons of focusing on getting a college degree and living at home while in community college.	No college degree. Earning less money for life! Having to move from family home at an earlier date.
A Drug/Alcohol Contract is incorporated into this Contract. (See my book *Let's Make a Contract: Getting Your Teen Through Substance Abuse.*)	To comply with the Drug/Alcohol Contract while living in caregiver's home.	First incident of breaking the Drug/Alcohol Contract negates this contract and teen must move out within 30 days.

CHAPTER 10

Teenage Self-Harm

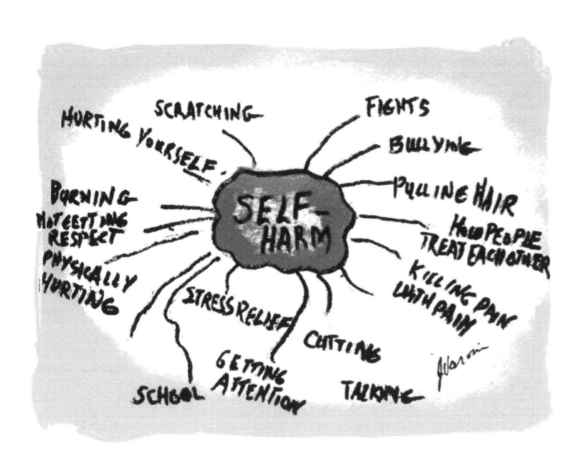

I can't tell you the number of times I have been called to the emergency department to evaluate a teen who has cut him/herself with a razor blade, scissors, a paperclip, or numerous other instruments. There are also those adolescents who burn themselves with matches, cigarettes, and other heated apparatus. Then there are those who pull out their own hair, punch holes in walls, overdose in a nonlethal way, bang their heads against walls, or create a variety of other practices to deliberately harm themselves. The parents are frantic and think that the cutting is a suicide attempt. Relatives of the teen who burns herself can't seem to understand the teen's actions at all. Teens are bandaged or sewn up. After medical care and a psychiatric evaluation to make sure the self-harm wasn't a suicide attempt, they go home with their parents and often the cycle continues. While the adults in the family don't like these practices, many have told me they grew to consider their teen's behavior an idiosyncrasy, "something they will outgrow." Sometimes this is actually true because for many teens, DSH (deliberate self-harm) represents a transient period of distress. However we decide to view DSH, any self-harm activity IS A SIGN OF AN UNHAPPY ADOLESCENT.

DSH, also called nonsuicidal self-injury (NSSI), is a way of expressing and living with deep distress and emotional pain (usually guilt, emptiness, self-loathing, sadness, and rage). It is a way people use to cope with problems and express feelings that can't put into words. DSH distracts from and helps release stress from perceived unsolvable obstacles. What is so difficult for nondeliberate self-harmers to understand is that performing the self-harm rituals temporarily makes one feel better. But then the pain returns, and the self-harm is repeated. It becomes an automatic coping mechanism for dealing with emotions and stress. It becomes an ingrained practice. It is an impulse disorder.

Most deliberate self-harm activities are done in secrecy and cause minor to moderate physical injury. DSH is learned from awareness of parents or schoolmates who self-harm. Some segments of the Goth and emo cults ritualize the practice of self-harm. DSH is more prevalent in females than in males. It can start as early as 11 or 12, but typically begins around age 14 and can continue well into adulthood. At these ages, preteens and teens don't have brains that have matured enough to help them to sort out other coping alternatives, and if one practices DSH as a coping mechanism long enough, pretty soon it becomes "normal."

Here are the main reasons that teens deliberately self-harm—as you review this list, consider if you can think of any teen who could possibly solve these issues by him/herself:

1. Eating disorders
2. History of physical, emotional, or sexual abuse
3. A cry for help
4. Belonging to a cult in which the practice of self-harm is considered "normal"
5. A symptom of psychiatric problems such as anxiety, depression, attention disorders, or bipolar disorder
6. Negative self-regard
7. Deliberate self-harm by friends
8. Conflicts with parents
9. Substance abuse

10. Being bullied
11. Concerns about sexual orientation issues
12. Impulsivity
13. A family history of suicidal behavior
14. Parental loss due to emotional distancing from parents and inconsistent parental warmth
15. Perceived loss of a significant other.

If you have a teen or young adult who is practicing NSSI, get him or her a psychiatric evaluation. The majority of teens who practice NSSI never get treatment and therefore the infliction of self-injury goes on and on into adulthood. Make sure that each of the items listed above are ruled out by the therapist until the underlying reasons for self-harm are discovered. Provide therapy to help your teen discover different coping mechanisms.

Is It a Suicide Attempt?

Many of the self-harming teens I have seen in the emergency department reported that they actually wanted to die. Why? They feel helpless and hopeless, they often blame themselves for family dynamics and/or they are recipients of negative role modeling. Having a nebulous desire to die is quite different from having suicidal thoughts that are accompanied by a plan and intent. Whether one's teen actively or passively wants to harm themselves, getting help is critical.

If YOU are NOT trained in how to handle suicidal threats or thoughts, call 911. If your teen tells you "I was just kidding," call 911 anyway. If your teen threatens to run away if you call for help, call 911 anyway.

What Can We Do to Help Our Teens?

It is crucial to get psychological help for our DSH teens. Make sure the therapist assesses for the function of the behavior and gets a commitment from your teen to try alternative behaviors.

Dialectical Behavior Therapy (DBT) for adolescents has been shown to be an effective treatment for those teens that practice DSH and are experiencing depression, hopelessness, suicidal ideation, and questioning their reasons for living. This therapy assists a teen in modulating their emotions, while providing skills with which to increase their interpersonal effectiveness and distress tolerance.

DBT is a lot of work. Therefore, in addition to this therapy, help your teen to explore other ways to distract from the ruminations that lead to self-harm. Make your help "out of the box" and fun. I know these techniques work because of the hundreds of patients who have provided me with positive feedback about the fun/weird/stupid/comical experiences they have had from trying these different deliberate self-harm ritual breakers:

1. *Counting whiskers:* Ever tried to count the whiskers on your furry pet? Get your pet and try to count their whiskers, and while you are doing this, attempt to focus on what is worrying or stressing you out. You can't focus on these two things at once. Counting whiskers breaks one's concentration on

the topic of worry. It helps offset the urge to self-harm and if practiced as a replacement for self-inflicted gestures, it can break the cycle. Remember, when counting whiskers, there are more of them than the ones on each side of the nose.

2. *The old ice cube trick:* Many of my patients have adopted the practice of putting an ice cube in each hand and holding them over the sink until they are experiencing physical discomfort. Then let go. The object is NOT to get frostbite, but rather to gauge when one is physically uncomfortable because their hands are so cold. The brain is not able to focus on stress, anxiety, cravings, etc., during physical discomfort. This technique helps to break self-harm rituals.

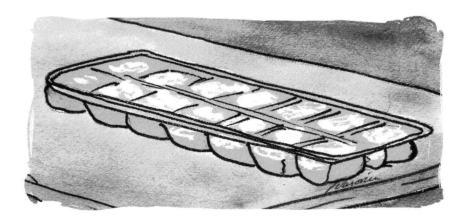

3. *Eyes open:* Many think that mindfulness meditation is helpful for those who have NSSI tendencies. Sometimes this is very contraindicated because the well-practiced ritualistically self-harming mind will focus on stress, or conflict or relationship problems. Focusing on a grounding technique with one's eyes open will help form a barrier between the unsolvable problem or ongoing emotion and the act of self-harm.

There are many "eyes open" grounding techniques. This is one that many teens like because they are the ones who select what objects to focus on.

Sit in a chair and select five things in the room to look at. Remember these five things. As you look at them again, imagine their temperature, then imagine their texture, see if they have any color in common, think of one thing you like about each of your selections. When you are done, see if you are still focused on the issue that was going to lead you to self-harm.

4. *Scrapbooking:* When I have suggested this idea to families I see in the ER, the teens often tell me, "That is the stupidest thing I have ever heard! I did that in kindergarten. That is soooooo lame!" When I hear this, and I often do, I never try to convince any teen that this might be a helpful way to offset their self-harm rituals and enable them to learn a different coping technique. Remember, self-harm rituals are shame-based behaviors that teens think will provide relief from overwhelming issues, impulses, and emotions. Here are some suggestions to make this more fun. Parents and relatives can join their teen in this exercise by making their own scrapbook beside them. Collect magazines, catalogues, and the like. Have glue, scissors, and paper that can be fastened into a scrapbook. Here are some ideas that have resonated with teens:

a. The holiday wish-list scrapbook
b. The car you want
c. Your dream scrapbook
d. Hot "chicks" and "dudes"
e. Outfits that are "cool"
f. Video games I'd like
g. New techie products
h. Animals
i. Skateboard stuff
j. Motorcycles
k. Making a baby album about yourself.
This list can go on forever.

Miss Goldie

5. *Loving the goldfish:* Nancy, a 15-year-old patient of mine, came up with this one. Due to a variety of allergies, she could not have a furry pet. She became very upset during a group where members were reporting on how many whiskers they counted on their pets and how the "counting whiskers" exercise had helped them overcome an urge to self-harm. Nancy was quite a creative teen. She had an 8-year-old goldfish (can you believe it?) whom she had named George. She decided that if she couldn't count whiskers she would count how many laps George made around his bowl in one minute. She set a timer and began counting. This helped her refocus and avoid her usual routine of scratching herself with a paperclip.

6. *Grocery shopping:* Make out your grocery list. Drive or send your teen to the grocery store. Lend them a credit card with the express (written) understanding that the credit card is for the groceries on the list and for NOTHING else.

7. *Omega-3:* There is current research that indicates that omega-3 along with therapy has achieved substantial reductions in symptoms of depression, tendencies to self-harm, suicidality, and daily stresses. Make sure you check with your teen's physician or psychiatrist before giving your teen omega-3 supplementation.

8. *Adult coloring books:* While coloring books date back to the 1880s, they have recently become a popular tool to assist with reductions in anxiety. They have become a part of the arsenal of self-soothing techniques. "Adult coloring" has been shown to distract one from ruminations, worry, and cravings for drugs/alcohol. It is a great stress reliever. For teens, we might want to find a coloring book that is about some interest of theirs.

9. *Paint by sticker:* These books are the latest on the market—great fun!

Remember, teens who self-harm are suffering from emotional pain. They need all the help we can give them. Sometimes, self-harm is a result of what is going on in a teen's family. As a parent, it is incumbent on us to seek help for the family also.

The following contract suggestion is meant to be discussed with your teen. Hopefully, it will help provide a safety net so your teen's fear of repercussion from their disclosure of DSH will be diminished. If your teen is scratching him/herself with a paperclip, this does not suggest a suicide attempt. If your teen is cutting with a razor blade, this suggests that medical care and a psychiatric evaluation might be in order. YOU will have to be the judge. Please err on the side of caution.

Contract to Intervene in Deliberate Self-Harm

Agreements	My Responsibilities	Consequences for Breaking Agreements
As your parents, we are dedicated to keeping you safe. If harming yourself through cutting, burning, etc., is the only way you can find relief for emotional distress, we will help you find other ways. There will be no deliberate self-harm (DSH) while you are living in the family home.	<u>Parents</u>: Be aware that some teens relieve emotional pain through DSH. <u>Teen</u>: Confide in your parent, or a safe person if you don't feel you can tell your parent, that you are engaging is deliberate self-harm activity.	<u>Parents</u>: If DSH is ignored long enough, it can become your teen's main coping technique with which to deal with strong emotions. <u>Teen</u>: You will not learn other ways of dealing with stress and other painful emotions. Your body will become permanently scarred.
<u>Parents</u>: If your teen confides in you about DSH behavior, there will be NO punishment, no shaming responses, no demeaning feedback. Such a disclosure will be greeted as phenomena to problem solve. <u>Teen</u>: We realize that telling your parents that you are engaging in DSH can be scary. Hopefully, this contract will help you to feel safe in making such a disclosure.	<u>Parents</u>: Listen to your teen without judgment. Ask questions: How long have you been doing this? How often do you cut (fill in the behavior)? How did you learn about this? Have you tried to stop? What does this behavior do for you? <u>Teen</u>: Tell you parents the absolute truth—it will assist them in helping you. THERE IS TO BE NO PUNISHMENT WHEN A TEEN DISCLOSES DSH.	<u>Parents</u>: Your teen will be reluctant to ask for help from you in the future. This will create a culture of secret keeping between you and your teen. <u>Teen</u>: You will teach yourself that self-harm is the only way to deal with your emotions.
<u>Parents</u>: We will help our teen by distracting him/her from self-harming behaviors. We will assist our teens with trying the techniques mentioned above. <u>Teen</u>: Be open to trying something new to relieve your frustrations and overwhelming emotions.	<u>Parents</u>: We will provide some of the items necessary to try the distracting techniques listed above. <u>Teen</u>: We will try some of the above distracting techniques and advise our parents which ones work the best for us.	<u>Parents</u>: You will strengthen your teen's desire to relieve strong emotions through their deliberate self-harm behavior. You will leave the DSH problem for your teen to solve—and this is a task your teen is not capable of doing by himself/herself. <u>Teen</u>: You will be stuck in a problem you cannot solve by yourself.
Parent: Will find a DBT therapist and take teen to and from therapy. Some DBT is free in the community. Teen: Will participate in DBT therapy and do the homework that is necessary for success.	**Dialectical Behavior Therapy (DBT)** Parent: Allow the therapist and your teen to engage in DBT therapy without your unrequested assistance. Respect the confidentiality your teen has with the therapist. <u>Teen</u>: Build a trusting relationship with your therapist and use the coping techniques you learn.	<u>Parents</u>: You will not be providing your teen with one of the best ways to diminish self-harm behavior and chances are, the DSH behavior will continue. Teen: You will be robbing yourself of the opportunity to learn better coping skills.
Most DSH behaviors are not suicide attempts—but some are. When in doubt, call 911.	**Suicide** Teen: Tell you parents if you are feeling hopeless. Parents: Call 911 and then call your therapist.	<u>Parents</u>: You could be putting your teen at risk. <u>Teen</u>: You could be putting your own life at risk.

Self-Harming Games that Teens Play

There is a segment of the teen population who engage in other types of self-harming behavior. These are often called "games," and unlike the NSSI rituals discussed above, these teen "games" are almost always life-threatening. The very fact that teens participate in them underscores the scientific truth that teen brains are not developed enough to weigh risk or to think out the consequences of their behavior. The "games" described below may seem unbelievable. From the perspective of a mature brain, that is certainly true. We may ask ourselves, "Who would ever do this?" But as we guardians of teens and young adults all know, taking risks, and joining in new and peer-accepted activities often clouds all judgment. I am sure that the "games" discussed below are not the only ones that enter into teen experience. New ones are being developed every day by our more creative and risk-taking teens. Be aware.

Alcohol Enemas

This is known as "butt chugging" and refers to the practice of inserting an alcohol-soaked tampon or a funnel-type of apparatus into the rectum. This leads to faster intoxication and it also neutralizes the body's ability to reject alcohol by vomiting.

Vodka Eyeballing

With the goal of getting drunk faster, this "party game" involves using an eye dropper to put vodka directly into the eye. Vodka eyeballing produces pain and can cause eye damage,

Hand Sanitizer

Because hand sanitizer has a greater concentration of alcohol than hard liquor, drinking it produces immediate intoxication and can lead to alcohol poisoning.

Pill Parties

The "admission ticket" to this party is bringing lots of prescription medication that is gotten by raiding the medicine cabinets of one's parents. Teens trade the pills with each other and often mix them with alcohol. Such mixtures can be deadly.

Skittling

Much like the pill party game, this one is often done in twosomes. Teens grab pills from the medicine cabinet, mix them up, and swallow a small and random handful. This game can be life-threatening.

The Purple Drink

This "drink" is a mixture of cough syrup, soda, and purple hard candies. Alcohol is an often added ingredient. Ingesting this mixture can lead to hallucinations, lethargy, and impairment of motor skills.

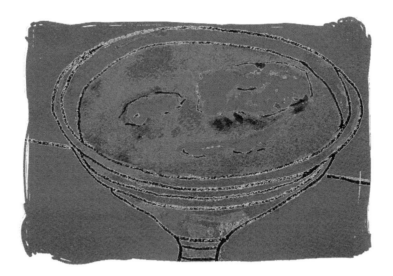

Car Surfing

Car surfing involves a teen standing or kneeling on the top of a moving vehicle. Obviously, this can lead to death.

The Choking Game

This game (also called "Space Monkey," and the "Pass Out Game") involves squeezing the neck or applying pressure to it which restricts the flow of oxygen and blood to the brain. When the compression is released, a high is produced by the reentry of blood and oxygen to the brain. This activity is practiced in a group or by oneself through using a belt, rope, or necktie to manually apply pressure. Teens can lose consciousness from playing this game and, within seconds, can damage their brain and central nervous system. Research indicates that this game is often played in conjunction with substance use.[15] Clues that your teen may be playing this game include bruises around the neck, frequent headaches, bloodshot eyes, and disorientation.

Teens seem to like to participate in "games" in which they can "win." They call these games "challenges." The idea of "winning" is showing one's friends that you can beat the challenge. The actual "win," however, is risking illness or death, another example of the teenage brain not being able to weigh the possible consequences of their actions.

---

[15] *http://abcnews.go.com/Health/study-percent-kids-play-choking-game/story?id=16144299.*

The Cinnamon Challenge

The players in this game swallow a teaspoon of cinnamon without taking a drink. This immediately dries out the mouth and can lead to violent coughing and vomiting. Cinnamon can also enter the lungs and lead to the necessity of using a respirator for breathing support.

The Ice and Salt Challenge

This is a game that has become popular with our younger teens. It is a challenge to see how much pain one can withstand. A participant wets an area of skin, covers it with table salt, and then presses an ice cube on the area. The salt provides an extremely fast transition from cold to below freezing. Of course, anyone taking this "challenge" will experience extreme pain. The "winner" of the challenge is the one who can take the pain the longest. Participants in this "game" can experience blistering, first- or second-degree burns, or frostbite.

Water Chugging

Drinking too much water is known as "hyperhydration." It can be deadly. Drinking too much water dilutes the sodium in the bloodstream, which can cause fluid imbalance in cells. Becoming hyperhydrated can lead to nausea, headaches, brain swelling, respiratory arrest, coma, and death.

The Gallon Challenge

In this "game," teens challenge each other to drink an entire gallon of milk and hold it in for an hour without vomiting. The stomach is unable to process an entire gallon of milk in one sitting, so the outcome of participating in this "game" is a severe case of vomiting, diarrhea, cramps, and bloating.

The Knockout Challenge

Like the Space Monkey game, the Knockout Challenge is an asphyxiation game. To participate in this "challenge," a teen rapidly inhales and exhales. This causes hyperventilation. While one teen is hyperventilating, another teen presses against his/her chest to inhibit air flow. The teen then loses consciousness.

30-Second Fight Game

Teens violently and aggressively have physical fights for 30 seconds while others watch. At the end of the 30-second bout, a winner is declared. Serious injuries can be a potential outcome of participating in this "game."

ABC Games

Using a sharp instrument like a fingernail or paperclip, one person digs at another person's skin while they list words beginning with each letter of the alphabet. Even though the skin breaks during the digging, the teen continues on in the game until they finish the alphabet or give up. This can invite infection, scarring, and even more serious outcomes if the sharp instrument in unclean.

Robotripping

This is a game in which a teen chugs an entire bottle of cough syrup to get high. DXM (dextromethorphan) is one of the main chemicals in many cough syrups, and it is this ingredient that causes the high. DXM induces hallucinations and in excessive amounts can cause death.

Sack-Tapping

An especially dangerous game, this involves punching someone in the testicles. This can lead to permanent injuries.

The Chubby Bunny

I was horrified one afternoon when I watched the host of a TV show playing this game with one of her guest stars. They thought it was funny. What a horrible role model for our teens and young adults. This "game" involves stuffing as many marshmallows in the mouth as possible and trying to say, "chubby bunny." One can choke to death from playing this game.

Ghost Train

To have "scary fun," teens drive their car, which is usually full of their friends, onto train tracks, then fog up the windows, with the idea that doing this will help them experience a ghost. Teens have died playing this game because they become unaware of approaching trains.

The Alcohol Binge

There are many alcohol drinking games. With most of them, the idea is to get drunk as fast as you can without passing out or vomiting. This can lead to alcohol poisoning and even death. Alcohol poisoning occurs when the amount of ethanol in a teenager's system exceed his/her body's ability to metabolize the chemical. There are too many teen alcohol games to list here. Beware. Teen parties are often centered on getting drunk and high.

Neknomination

This is a game that can be played on the Internet. It requires a teen to post proof of completing a drunken dare on YouTube, Facebook, and Twitter and then nominate another player to do something equally dangerous such as disrobing in public, driving while drunk, consuming toxic concoctions of alcohol and other substances, going car surfing, and the like.

Huffing or Dusting

Teens inhale the compressed gas used in computer keyboard duster spray or other common household products to get high. This practice can become addictive and lead to serious injury, brain damage, or death.

Mumblety Peg

Players spread their fingers on a table and then stab at the spaces between them as quickly as possible with a pocketknife. This game often ends up with participants needing stitches.

The Deodorant Challenge

This "game" originated in England. As like many fads, I predict it will be heading west. This game involves spraying deodorant on the skin and the "challenge" is to see how long one can keep spraying it without stopping. Deodorant is not the problem. Rather it is the aerosol spray that quickly cools on the skin and turns into frostbite. This can render second-degree burns. YouTube is instructing tweens and teens how to enter this "challenge."

The Tide Pod Challenge

This started in 2017 with teens posting memes and videos of themselves stuffing their mouths with laundry detergent pods and chewing them up. The "challenge" is to see how many pods one can stuff into one's mouth, chew up and swallow. This "game" can cause chemical burns, coma, seizure, pulmonary edema, and respiratory arrest.

Dripping

Dripping involves e-cigarettes. It is practiced by "dripping" liquid nicotine onto the exposed heating coils of the e-cigarette to produce a thicker cloud of vapor. This releases a higher level of toxins, including formaldehyde.

The Duct Tape Challenge

This "challenge" involves duct taping the participant to a pole so they have to break free. Teens have allowed themselves to be taped to items which are off the ground. Thus, when they break free they are at risk for breaking bones and other injuries.

Vampire Biting

Taken from the Twilight series, teens have developed a new way of kissing—they "love bite." Teens claim that participating with this practice makes them feel closer to each other. The problem is that skin is often broken and human saliva can be even more dangerous than animal bites because of the bacteria and viruses it contains.

Condom Snorting

Really? What will our teens think of next? This "game" played by snorting a condom through one's nose and pulling it out of his/her mouth. The problem is, the player could choke to death.

Protection

Protecting one's teen from self-harm games can be a sensitive endeavor. We parents don't want to go through a list of dangerous games with our teen because the power of suggestion can be enormous and lead one's teen to try something that sounds kewl and that they have never heard of before. Can't you imagine your teen going to school and telling a friend about the "neatest game I've ever heard of—we must try it! I even heard about it from my MOM!"?

How do we protect without inviting our teen to explore ideas that could harm them? NOT by having a contract. What would such a document say? You will not play Neknomination? Any inquiring teen would quickly look that up on the Internet and might be off and running with the idea at school. The following is a list of some ideas that could assist us in getting our teens to adulthood with as little self-harm as possible:

1. Monitor the Internet! It doesn't matter that your teen won't like this. It doesn't matter that you will be accused of not respecting their privacy. The Internet contains literally thousands of videos and sets of instructions about how to perform NSSI and how to play teen "challenges." These pieces of information tend to normalize such activities and make them seem fun and/or pleasurable.
2. Be on the lookout for evidence that your teen has been involved in a self-harm game. For example, are there bruises in the neck or eye area? Are there any cuts on hands and fingers, arms, and legs?
3. After spending time alone does your teen complain of headaches? This could be a sign of participation in any of the activities listed above.
4. If you discover that your teen is participating in any of these nonintentional suicidal behaviors or teen "challenges," definitely talk to them about it. Create your own contract. The contract on the next page is offered to give parents some idea about how to approach creating a safety net for your teen.

Self-Harming Game Contract

Agreements	My Responsibilities	Consequences for Breaking Agreements
We have discovered that you and some of your friends have been playing the choking game. We love you, and it is our responsibility to keep you safe from being involved in activities that could unintentionally put your life at risk. We know you might not like this contract but it is the best way we can think of to protect you. If you have contributions you would like to make to this contract, we welcome them.	Guardians: Address this issue openly with your teen in a non-shaming manner. Inquire (without judgment) what they liked about the choking game. Ask if there any other activities your teen enjoys as much as they like the choking game. Question how your teen came to learn about the "game," and learn how many times they have engaged in it. Ask your teen about how he/she feels about continued participation in the choking game.	Guardians: Ignoring this topic will enable your teen to continue to put his/her life at risk.
If you press for a promise not to play the choking game anymore, your teen could agree just to satisfy you and escape the conversation. Guardian: Protect your teen from poor judgment by making sure alone time with or without friends is limited.	Guardians: Establish a house rule that bedroom doors are kept open at all times. When your teen's door is closed for changing clothing purposes, check on them. Teen: Keep your bedroom door open at all times except when dressing, which will take about five minutes maximum. Set your clothes out the night before you will wear them.	Guardian: Alone time provides opportunities to engage in NSSI. Teen: If you choose to ignore this agreement, the door will be removed from your room for 30 days.
Teen: Activities with friends who come over to visit will take place in the family area of our home. Guardian: When your teen has friends over, remove yourself from the family area for a short period of time so they will not be "hindered" by having you in their space for the entire visit.	Teen: Taking your friend to your room will result in your friend being taken home. Guardian: Give your teen some privacy while they are in the family area. Take your teen and his/her friend out to do an activity.	Teen: If you decide to go to your room with your friend, or to go to any other private area in our home, no friends will be invited over for one week. Guardian: You will teach your teen that you are not willing to go the extra mile (via supervision) to protect him/her from engaging in NSSI activities.
Guardian: When teen is invited to friend's homes, check to make sure an adult is home. Discuss the choking (and other self-harm) "games" with the supervising adult. You don't have to "out" your teen's past behavior. Share your home guidelines with the friend's guardian.	Guardian: Educate the guardians of your teen's friends about DSH. Make sure that when your teen visits a friend's home adults will be present.	Guardian: You will not be protecting your teen from poor judgment and participation in DSH "games." Action could save a life.
Teen: Even though it may be difficult due to peer pressure or your desire to get "high," you agree to not engage in dangerous "games" or "challenges."	Teen: Stay away from activities that could put your life at risk.	Teen: Increased supervision by your guardian for two weeks. This includes accompanying you to social activities to check them for safety.

CHAPTER 11

Tattoos, Body Piercings, and Ear Stretching

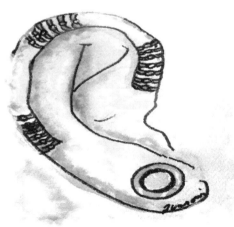

Tattoos and piercings have become growing fads with adults and teens alike. Ear stretching (also known as ear gauging) is also a fad, albeit a less popular one. Many adults have tattoos and piercings. It is mainly teens and young adults who lean toward ear stretching. Caregivers of teens and young adults, each of you need to decide what your position is on these issues! Before deciding, here are some questions to ask yourself:

1. How will having a tattoo, piercings, or enlarged ear lobes affect my teen's future?
2. Is there a hidden significance or meaning to tattoos, piercings, and gauged ears?
3. Do I want to allow my teen/young adult to follow any of these particular fads?
4. Are tattoos, piercings, or ear stretching reversible? If so, what is the process?

Let's explore these three fads, one by one, and after doing so, every reader should be able to make a decision on how to guide their teen. We'll start with the one about which the least is known.

Ear Stretching

Ear stretching, also known as gauging, has been around for centuries. Traditionally, enlarging one's ear lobes has been considered a body enhancement, a body alteration to enhance one's beauty. It was mainly practiced by indigenous people around the world, and has recently become somewhat popular in modern cultures. Currently, ear stretching is often associated with certain subcultures or social cliques such as punks and emos. It provides a sign of affiliation and belonging.

How does one stretch an ear lobe? This is a slow process because it is important to avoid any tearing. One begins by progressively enlarging a healed piercing with larger and larger pieces of jewelry until the earlobe is stretched to the desired size. One can have this professionally done or one can buy a kit to do it oneself. It is important to note that unlike a regular piercing that will heal itself over time when jewelry is removed, the larger hole created by ear stretching will not heal itself. A usually uncomplicated plastic surgery becomes the only method of ear lobe restoration.

For those who want immediate stretched lobes, there's dermal punching. This is a procedure done with a round, very sharp blade. It creates perfectly round holes and is customarily used in the medical field to take biopsy samples.

A flesh tunnel is a type of jewelry used when one has stretched the earlobe to the point where one can see through the hole. They are made of a variety of materials including wood, bone, and steel. The metal flesh tunnels are reminiscent of grommets which are placed in a hole to insulate the outer material from being torn. Ear plugs are solid and do not allow the hole in the earlobe to be seen through.

There can be some risky side effects of ear stretching. This practice can invite *infection* because ear stretching continuously opens new wounds in areas that have previously healed. Bacteria can enter the body when using unclean gauges or instruments to enlarge the flesh tunnel. This can lead to pain, scarring, and infection. Keloids can form, fibrous growths that can be painful and disfiguring and require treatment by steroids. Keloids can become a chronic problem because they often recur after removal. Along with the possibility of infection and keloids, the *blood supply to the ear lobe* can be altered from gauging too quickly. This can lead to separation of the earlobe from where it is attached to the side of the head. Plastic surgery becomes necessary to repair this. *Pain* is the common denominator; not only from the risky side effects, but each time one inserts a larger gauge into the ear, one will experience a considerable amount of pain.

Those with gauged ears do not go unnoticed. For many, a reaction of repugnance is the first response. Consider the possible long-range ramifications for your teen or young adult before you give in to pressure to support this practice.

Body Piercing

For centuries, ear and nose piercings have been practiced by males and females. Various ancient cultures have long histories of lip, tongue, nipple, and genital piercings. In Western culture the piercing of sites other than ears became popular with some of the subcultures of the 1970s. Body piercing became more mainstream beginning in the 1990s.

Why has body piercing become a trend with teens and young adults? There is perhaps a range of reasons. Body piercings are done for self-expression, for sexual pleasure, to rebel against cultural norms, or for aesthetic value. Some get piercings because they like the feel of the needle going through their skin. Throughout history many types of body piercings carried with them a special meaning. For example, in 16th-century India a piercing in the left nostril of a female is supposed to make childbirth easier and lessen menstrual pain. It can also indicate submissiveness. In ancient Rome, some of the soldiers thought that piercing their nipples was a way of expressing their strength and virility. In Borneo men often pierced their genitals for sexual enhancement reasons. In contemporary culture, meanings are also attached to various types of piercings. The following is not intended to be a compendium of the history or meaning of different piercings on the body. It is simply general information to give the reader some areas of consideration if your teen/or young adult wants a piercing in a particular place on their body.

1. **Ear piercing** is probably the most popular and accepted kind of piercing.

For men, piercing of the right ear lobe indicates one is gay. The right ear is called the "gay ear." Piercings on the left ear indicate one is straight, and when men pierce both ears this also suggests that they are straight. Currently, so many men have their ears pierced the significance is questionable.

For women, piercing of the ear is usually a function of wanting to adorn that area of the body.

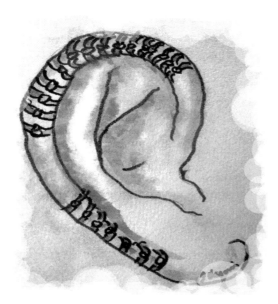

2. **Tongue piercing** studs indicate more pleasure for the recipient during oral sex.

3. **Lip piercing**

Labret: a piercing that accommodates adornments attached to the lips. The types of labrets refer to the positioning of the piercing on the lip(s):

Snakebite: two piercings evenly separated on the right and left side of the lower lip.

Spider bites: a pair of piercings close together on the bottom lip.

Angel bites: like a snake bite but on both sides of the upper lip.

Madonna: piercing on the upper right side of one's lip.

Monroe: a piercing on the upper left side of one's lip.

Medusa: a piercing done on the philtrum region just below the septum of the nose. If this piercing is done incorrectly, it can alter the face symmetry.

Vertical: a piercing just below the lip that comes out on the middle of the lower lip.

Meanings of lips piercings seem to vary from individual to individual. Some think that having a lip pierced on the right side denotes a straight person and having the piercing on the left side indicates someone is gay. It seems, however, that there are no set meanings when it comes to lip piercings.

A word of caution: Healing from lip piercings can be problematical because of the bacteria in and around the mouth areas.

4. **Nose piercing** has become very popular with many teens and young adults. As with all body piercings, there is a variety of choices one can make when considering piercing one's nose:

Double or triple nostril piercing: two or three holes on the top crease of the nose are created for jewelry.

Septum piercing: piercing the cartilage division of the nostril.

Bridge piercing: piercing the bridge of the nose for placement of a curbed or circular barbell type of jewelry.

Nasallang: a tri-nasal piercing that goes through both nostrils and the septum.

5. **Navel piercing** is located in or near the navel but usually through its upper rim. While this type of piercing used to signify a type of personal identity, youth, and rebellion, it has currently evolved to be simply a fashion trend.

6. **Nipple piercing** reportedly makes one's nipples more sensitive and provides constant stimulation.

7. **Genital piercings** come in many varieties and all are purported to increase sexual pleasure. For some, piercing is part of an S-M lifestyle or relationship or is incorporated into S-M play.

Tattooing

Tattoos, also known as body art, are permanent designs that are created by inserting pigment into punctures in the skin. They have myriad meanings. For some, tattoos have a spiritual meaning, for others they are a way of making a tribute to a loved one, and yet for others they make a statement about a way of thinking or a belief. With research from StylesAtLife.com's "100 Most Popular Tattoo

Designs and Their Meanings" and from TheOdysseyOnline.com's "20 Small Tattoos with Big Meanings," the following will provide a small survey of the vast possibilities of the meanings of tattoos.

The semicolon tattoo has come to symbolize the Semicolon Project, which is a nonprofit organization dedicated to supporting people dealing with various forms of mental challenges. The semicolon represents an unended sentence. It has become used as a metaphor for a life that one has chosen to continue, not end. The semicolon has evolved into a symbol for hope and continuation. To quote the project's website, "Drawing a semicolon on your wrist can act as a constant reminder and prevention strategy to help you come to your recovery; after all, you are the author of your life and you should choose not to end it."

SEMICOLON TATTOO

- A barbed wire tattoo can indicate that one has been to prison.
- A red rose is a symbol for romance.
- The phoenix symbolizes that one has risen from ashes and has renewed their life.
- Praying hands often represent faith.
- Sugar skulls are associated with the Mexican Day of the Dead and symbolize a way of honoring loved ones who have died.
- Nautical tattoos became first became popular with sailors. If certain tattoos were put on their feet, the belief was that they would not drown while at sea.
- Hearts with swords through them suggest that one has been betrayed.
- Star tattoos are symbols for truth and hope. Stars are the light that shines through the darkness, and thus a star tattoo reminds its wearer that they can fight against darkness and find a new path.
- Angel tattoos provide symbols for guidance and protection.

- Wing tattoos usually have a spiritual significance of protection and guidance.
- Tribal tattoos are usually revered for their intricate artwork.
- Fairy tattoos are thought to symbolize people who wish to keep their inner child alive and active.
- *Lux in tenebris* means "light in darkness."
- Anchor tattoos symbolize strength and stability no matter how difficult things get.
- *Ad maiora* means "Toward greater things." It suggests the wearer wishes for more success in all things in life.
- The lotus flower symbolizes rising above adversity.
- The teardrop tattoo can be a symbol that one has done prison time or was raped while serving a sentence.

Along with the assorted meanings of tattoos, there are various placement issues. Tattoos on feet and hands tend to fade more quickly due to being areas of heavy use. Sun exposure also fades tattoos. Midsection tattoos are affected by aging and often lose their shape. There are back, shoulder, bicep, chest, calf, neck, face, and rib tattoos. There are what is called "sleeves" that can cover either half or the entire arm. In working with one's teen, it is critical to determine where, how big, and what type of tattoo they wish. Some tattoos indicate gang membership, and one wouldn't want one's teen to unintentionally select a gang emblem.

Tattoos have become quite popular in contemporary society. If our teen/young adult wants a tattoo, and there are no objections to their desire, be aware that tattoos are PERMANENT and eventually tattoo wearers might want to have them removed. Today, the most popular way of tattoo removal is through using Q-switched lasers. Through a series of treatments, high intensity laser-supplied light beams break up the pigment colors of the tattoo. Complete success varies from person to person. WebMD suggests that one find a reputable dermatologist or cosmetic surgery center to perform tattoo removal procedures.

There is evidence that getting tattoos can become addictive. They can produce adrenaline rushes; they can stimulate endorphin production thereby producing a "natural high." They can become a substitute for cutting or burning one's self. Be aware of exactly why your teen wants a tattoo. It could be as simple as wanting to belong to the "tattoo culture," or there could be other reasons behind their desire. Sometimes teens and young adults want a tattoo to fill an inner void or because they feel inadequate.

As guardians of our teens and young adults, we have to decide what our guidelines are going to be. Tattooing, piercings, and ear stretching all used to belong to our subcultures. Now these forms of expression are becoming more common and are often received without judgment. If your teen wants one of these forms of "self-expression," it will be necessary for you to be specific about the where, when, how many, cost, and placement.

Houston

Houston was a tall, lanky, musically inclined senior in high school. His friends defined him as "kewl," because he played a "mean bass," and he was a master rapper. Given his reputation as a performer with great potential, Houston also wanted to look the part. His mother had hopes of Houston going to college. He wanted to try out for *The Voice* and get a recording contract. In order to win this competition, Houston felt he had to look the part. He wanted more of that "gangsta" look instead of his (to quote him) "everyday, boring, wannabe self." Houston felt that to win *The Voice* he would have to stand out not only musically and vocally, but physically. And thus began the arguments with Houston's parents, Gayle and Bernard.

Day after day, Houston would come home from jamming at school and beg to be able to get a piercing and a tattoo. He just knew it would help his music career. He struck a bargain with his dad that if he brought his grades up, Bernard would allow him to "get the stuff needed to help my music career." To Houston's father, that meant a tattoo and maybe an ear piercing. To Houston, that had a different meaning.

Sure enough, at the end of the first half of his senior year, Houston brought home his report card; all of his grades had improved. Bernard handed over his credit card and told his son how proud of him he was. He looked Houston in the eye and said, "Honey, you are a great son. You have earned this reward. Go get the tattoo and piercing that you think would help you make your dreams come true. You are so talented. I want to support you. Have fun and I'll look forward to seeing you when you come home."

Six hours later, Houston walked through the front door. Bernard, who was drinking a mug of coffee, dropped his cup on the carpet. There was Houston—with two piercings in his bottom lip; three tear tattoos descending under his right eye; uncountable piercings on his right ear, one in his left ear, a dagger on the top of his forearm, a bar through his septum, and a star next to his left eye. Bernard was flabbergasted! He couldn't believe his eyes! There was his beloved son! In Bernard's eyes, Houston had ruined himself. Upon hearing the commotion in the living room, Gayle entered to see what was going on. When she saw Houston's additions she screamed. "Houston!" she bellowed, "What have you done?" Houston was angry at his parent's responses. "What is your problem? Dad gave me his credit card and told me to go get what I needed to forward my career! And here you are all mad!" "How much did all this cost?" asked Bernard. "Sixteen hundred dollars," replied Houston.

Gayle glared at Bernard. "Is this true?" she asked in a cold voice. Bernard hung his head. "I never thought that Houston would do a face tattoo or pierce his lips much less his nose! I just thought he'd get something on his arm and maybe an ear piercing."

A specific contract will help parents delineate what they mean. Surprises like Gayle's and Bernard's can ruin trust. For Houston, he did what his father said he could do: use his own discretion to "get the stuff needed to help my music career." Bernard had thought his son would have sense enough to maybe pierce his ear and get a small tattoo. Gayle was angry because this was not a family decision and she had not been included in the agreement. Everyone felt betrayed. When this happens, there can be negative ramifications that can echo through family relations for decades.

Don't let this happen to you. If you decide to allow your teen to stretch his/her ear, or to get a piercing, or to have body art, make a contract!

If ear gauging, piercing, and tattoos are OK with a teen's parent(s), then be specific. For example: Houston may have one tattoo on his left bicep. It is not to be larger than two inches by two inches. Discuss the content of the tattoo so your teen doesn't inadvertently walk away with a gang or prison symbol.

Self-Harming Game Contract

Agreements	My Responsibilities	Consequences for Breaking Agreements
Parents(s): We love you and want you to have a successful life. To support you in this, there will be no ear stretching, tattooing, or piercings until you are independent from us and are supporting yourself.	Parent(s): Be clear about your expectations and the guidelines around tattooing, piercings, and ear gauging. Teen: Abide by the family guidelines regarding tattooing, piercings, and ear stretching.	Teen: Any tattoo, piercing, or ear gauging not done with permission of parent(s) will be immediately removed. Cost of these removals will be loaned by parent(s) and reimbursed to them by teen through earnings at a job and holiday/birthday gifts of money. Parent(s): Front the cost of tattoo, piercing, and gauging removal, and collect repayment. Keep a list of payments made by your teen.
Parent(s): We consider this a serious breach of family trust and therefore we cannot trust you with other things that require good judgment. We cannot trust you with driving a car, being home alone, having a cell phone, or having a bedroom door. Teen: By refusing to remove ear gauges, piercings, and tattoos, you are choosing to not be trusted and all the consequences that come with that.	**Refusing to Remove Them** Parents: Enforce the consequences.	Parent(s): To not enforce consequences is to give tacit permission for those things you say are "not OK." It gives permission to your teen to disrespect family guidelines. Teen: You are signing up for not driving, not having a cell phone or a bedroom door, and not being home alone.
Teen: Refusal to remove body adornments will mean you are choosing not to drive.	**The Car** Parent(s): Do not drive your teen anywhere—no matter what!	Teen: You will have to get to school and to your job or sports events on your own.
Parent(s): Will hire a babysitter or ask a relative to be with teen when they can't be home with him/her.	**Home Alone** Parent(s): Find available people to be home with your teen. If you can't find a sitter for your teen, take him/her with you.	Parent(s): Ignoring any part of any contract you make with your teen will teach him/her that your contracts don't really mean anything.
No cell phone No bedroom door Teen: Your privacy and your communications will become limited.	Parent: Once the unwanted body adornments are removed or taken out, all lost privileges are returned to teen.	Parents: Negotiating on any contract you have made teaches your teen that your contracts are negotiable. This can reward teen nagging, arguing, and other methods used to wear down the parent(s).

NOTE: All contracts in this book are available in electronic form to download, modify, and print.

For more information:
www.letsmakeacontract.com/contracts-th.html

Appendix A:
Sample 30-Day Notice to Quit

THIRTY-DAY NOTICE TO QUIT
TO:

_____

AND ALL OTHERS IN POSSESSION:

YOU ARE HEREBY NOTIFIED that pursuant to (name of state) Civil Code Section (find this code number online), the tenancy from month to month under which you hold the possession of the hereinafter described premises is terminated THIRTY (30) days after service on you of this notice.

YOU ARE FURTHER REQUIRED to quit and deliver up the possession of the hereinafter described premises to the Landlord/Agent who is authorized to receive possession of the same on or before the expiration of said THIRTY (30) days period.

YOU ARE FURTHER NOTIFIED that it is the purpose and intent of this Notice to terminate said tenancy at the expiration of said THIRTY (30) day period, and that if at the expiration of said period you fail to quit said premises and deliver up possession of the same, legal proceedings will be instituted for an unlawful detainer against you to recover possession of said premises, to declare said lease or rental agreement forfeited, and to recover damages for the unlawful detention of said premises.

The premises are located at: _____

Date: _____

LANDLORD/AGENT

State law permits former tenants to reclaim abandoned personal property left at the former address of the tenant, subject to certain conditions. You may or may not be able to reclaim property without incurring additional costs, depending on the cost of storing the property and the length of time before it is reclaimed. In general, these costs will be lower the sooner you contact your former landlord after being notified that property belonging to you was left behind after you moved out.

These forms are easily found online.

Appendix B: Love and Sex Abstinence[16]

Teaching abstinence is not only very popular; it also makes sense. Social science data show that teens who abstain from sex do substantially better on a wide range of outcomes. For example, teens who abstain from sex are less likely to be depressed and to attempt suicide; to experience STDs; to have children out-of-wedlock; and to live in poverty or welfare dependence as adults. Finally, teens who delay sexual activity are more likely to have stable and enduring marriages as adults.

Facts on American Teens' Sources of Information About Sex[17]

Sex, Pregnancy, and Abortion

- Although only 13% of U.S. teens have had sex by age 15, most initiate sex in their late teen years. By their 19th birthday, seven in 10 teen men and teen women have had intercourse.
- Between 1988 and 2006–2010, the proportion of never-married teens aged 15–17 who had ever engaged in sexual intercourse declined from 37% to 27% among females, and from 50% to 28% among males. During the same period, among teens aged 18–19, that proportion declined from 73% to 63% among females, and 77% to 64% among males.
- The pregnancy rate among young women has declined steadily, from 117 pregnancies per 1,000 women aged 15–19 in 1990 to 68 per 1,000 in 2008.
- The majority (86%) of the decline in the teen pregnancy rate between 1995 and 2002 was the result of dramatic improvements in contraceptive use, including an increase in the proportion of teens using a single method of contraception, an increase in the proportion using multiple methods simultaneously and a substantial decline in nonuse. Just 14% of the decline is attributable to decreased sexual activity.
- Of the approximately 750,000 teen pregnancies that occur each year, 82% are unintended. Fifty-nine percent end in birth and more than one-quarter end in abortion.
- In 2009, there were 39.1 births per 1000 women aged 15–19, marking a historic low in the birthrate. This rate represents a 37% decline from the peak rate of 61.8 in 1991.

---

[16] *"Teenage Sexual Abstinence and Academic Achievement," presented at the Ninth Annual Abstinence Clearinghouse Conference, August, 2005 by Robert Rector Kirk A. Johnson, PhD, of the Heritage Foundation in Washington, DC.*
[17] *The Guttmacher Institute, February 2012. https://www.guttmacher.org/sites/default/files/pdfs/pubs/FB-Teen-Sex-Ed.pdf.*

- The 2008 teenage abortion rate was 17.8 abortions per 1,000 women. This figure was 59% lower than its peak in 1988, but 1% higher than the 2005 rate.
- Compared with their Canadian, English, French, and Swedish peers, U.S. teens have a similar level of sexual activity, but they are more likely to have shorter and less consistent sexual relationships, and are less likely to use contraceptives, especially the pill or dual methods.
- The United States continues to have one of the highest teen pregnancy rates in the developed world (68 per 1,000 women aged 15–19 in 2008)—more than twice that of Canada (27.9 per 1,000) or Sweden (31.4 per 1,000).
- Every year, roughly nine million new STIs occur among teens and young adults in the United States. Compared with rates among teens in Canada and Western Europe, rates of gonorrhea and chlamydia among U.S. teens are extremely high.

Condom Use As Reported By Sexually Active Students in Grades 9 Through 12, by Gender and Grade, 2013

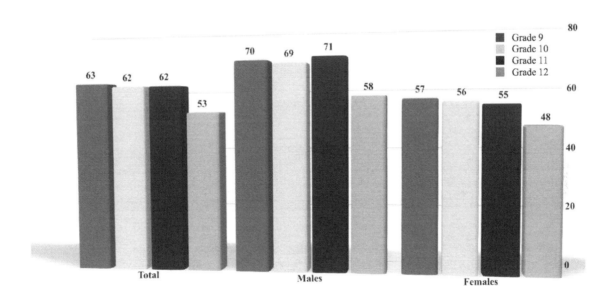

Students who have had sexual intercourse in the three months preceding this survey.
Source: Centers for Disease Control and Prevention (CDC). (2014). 1991-2013 High School Youth Risk Behavior Survey Data. Accessed on 07/22/2014. Available at http://nccd.cdc.gov/youthonline/.

Percentage of Sexually Active Females in Grades 9 Through 12 Who Reported Using Birth Control Pills at Most Recent Intercourse, by Gender and Grade, 2013

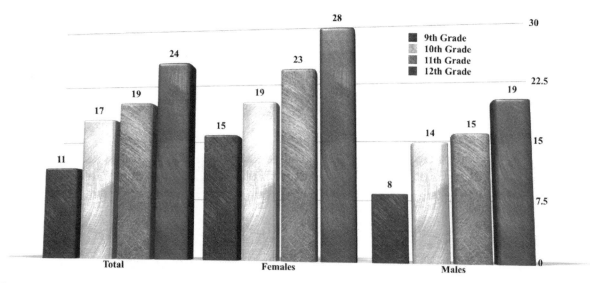

Students who have had sexual intercourse in the three months preceding this survey.
Source: Centers for Disease Control and Prevention (CDC). (2014). 1991-2013 High School Youth Risk Behavior Survey Data. Accessed on 07/22/2014. Available at http://nccd.cdc.gov/youthonline/.

Statistics for Teen Sexual Behavior in High School
Teen Pregnancy Outcomes, 2010
The majority of teen pregnancies end in birth.

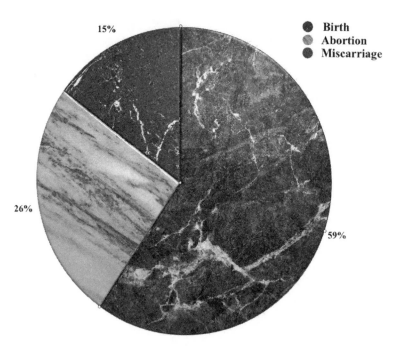

Source: https://www.guttmacher.org/fact-sheet/american-teens-sexual-and-reproductive-health.

Some Statistics Regarding Teen Sex

Childbearing

- In 2011, there were 334,000 births among girls aged 19 or younger, representing 8% of all U.S. births.
- Most births among teen mothers are first births. Eighteen percent are second or higher-order births.
- Nearly all teen births are nonmarital—89% in 2011, up from 79% in 2000. Yet, over the last several decades, the share of all nonmarital births that are among teenagers has been declining, from 52% in 1975 to 18% in 2011.
- In 2011, there were 31 births per 1,000 women aged 15–19; this rate marked a 50% decline from the peak rate of 62 reached in 1991.

Fatherhood

- Most teen males report that they would be very upset (47%) or a little upset (34%) if they got someone pregnant, while the remaining 18% report that they would be pleased or a little pleased.
- Teen fatherhood rates vary considerably by race. In 2010, the rate among black males aged 15–19 who became fathers (29 per 1,000) was more than twice that among whites (14 per 1,000).
- The rate of teen fatherhood declined 36% between 1991 and 2010, from 25 to 16 per 1,000 males aged 15–19. This decline was far more substantial among blacks than among whites (50% vs. 26%) and about half of the rate among teen girls.

Abortion

- Women aged 15–19 had 157,450 abortions in 2010. About 5% of all abortions are obtained by minors.
- The reasons teens most frequently give for having an abortion are that they are concerned about how having a baby would change their lives, cannot afford a baby now, and do not feel mature enough to raise a child.
- As of May 2014, laws in 38 states required that a minor seeking an abortion involve her parents in the decision.

Source: https://www.guttmacher.org/sites/default/files/pdfs/pubs/FB-ATSRH.pdf.

Appendix C: Contract for Loaning and Borrowing Property

Loan Agreement

Name of Lender: _____

Address of Lender: _____

Phone Number of Lender: _____

This agreement is for the loan of a _____ which is valued at $_____ to

Name of Borrower: _____

Address of Borrower: _____

Phone Number of Borrower: _____

Return Date: _____

Return Time: _____

If the borrowed item is lost, damaged, or stolen, or not returned for any other reason, it is agreed that the borrower is responsible for replacing the loaned item with one of similar quality and age or to give the lender the money to purchase a replacement item of the same make and quality as the one loaned. It is the borrower's responsibility to provide the lender with research in writing that establishes value. This research shall be from two places that sell the borrowed item.

Agreed Lender: _____

Agreed Borrower: _____

Appendix D: Values Template

Most Important Values	Somewhat Important Values	Unimportant Values

Bibliography

"About the Goth Youth Subculture." Center for Mental Health in Schools at UCLA. Accessed April 30, 2016. http://smhp.psych.ucla.edu/pdfdocs/youth/goth.pdf.

Agrella, Ronald. "12 Dangerous 'Games' Your Children Might Play." Safe Bee. March 16, 2015. Accessed May 1, 2016. http://www.safebee.com/family/12-dangerous-games-your-children-might-play.

Allen, Jae. "Reasons People Practice Ear Stretching." Livestrong. September 27, 2015. Accessed May 1, 2016. http://www.livestrong.com/article/340105-reasons-people-practice-ear-stretching/.

Brausch, Amy M., Kristina M. Decker, and Andrea G. Hadley. "Risk of Suicidal Ideation in Adolescents with both Self-Asphyxial Risk-Taking Behavior and Non-Suicidal Self-Injury." *Suicide and Life-Threatening Behavior* 41, no. 4 (2011): 424-434.

Carlie, Mike. "Into the Abyss: A Personal Journey into the World of Street Gangs: Part 6: The Gang Culture." Missouri State. 2002. Accessed April 30, 2016. http://people.missouristate.edu/michaelcarlie/what_i_learned_about/gangs/culture.htm.

Carlie, Mike. "The Structure of Gangs." Into the Abyss: A Personal Journey into the World of Street Gangs. 2002. Accessed July 24, 2016. http://people.missouristate.edu/michaelcarlie/what_i_learned_about/gangs/structure_of_gangs.htm.

Centers for Disease Control and Prevention (CDC). (2014). 1991-2013 High School Youth Risk Behavior Survey Data. Accessed on 07/22/2014. Available at http://nccd.cdc.gov/youthonline/.

"Emo Scene Community Lifestyle & Culture." So Emo. February 09, 2011. Accessed April 30, 2016. http://www.soemo.co.uk/emo lifestyle.php.

Farrell, Kirby. "If Tattoos Could Talk." *Psychology Today*. October 14, 2013. Accessed May 1, 2016. https://www.psychologytoday.com/blog/swim-in-denial/201310/if-tattoos-could-talk.

Fergusson, David M., L. John Horwood, and Annette L. Beautrais. "Is sexual orientation related to mental health problems and suicidality in young people?" *Archives of General Psychiatry* 56, no. 10 (1999): 876-880.

"Frequently Asked Questions About Gangs." National Gang Center. Accessed April 30, 2016. https://www.nationalgangcenter.gov/about/FAQ.

"Gay Ear." Urban Dictionary. Accessed May 1, 2016. http://www.urbandictionary.com/define.php?term=Gay Ear.

Grabianowski, Ed. "How Street Gangs Work." How Stuff Works. Accessed April 30, 2016. http://people.howstuffworks.com/street-gang.htm.

Greenblatt, Janet C. "Patterns of Alcohol Use among Adolescents and Associations with Emotional and Behavioral Problems. OAS Working Paper." (2000).

Harrison, Siobhan. "The Popularity and Pitfalls of Ear Stretching." Web MD. Accessed May 1, 2016. http://www.webmd.boots.com/healthy-skin/features/ear-stretching.

Henderson, James, and Charles M. Malata. "Surgical Correction of the expanded earlobe after ear gauging." *Aesthetic Plastic Surgery* 34, no. 5 (2010): 632-633.

Howell, James C. "Youth Gangs: An Overview. Juvenile Justice Bulletin. Youth Gang Series." *Juvenile Justice Bulletin* (1998).

Johnstone, Healther A., and John F. Marcinak. "Sibling abuse: Another component of domestic violence." *Journal of Pediatric Nursing* 12, no. 1 (1997): 51-54.

Katz, Kenneth A., and Robin L. Toblin. "Language matters: Unintentional strangulation, strangulation activity, and the 'choking game'." *Archives of Pediatrics & Adolescent Medicine* 163, no. 1 (2009): 93-94.

Kaufman, Miriam. "Adolescent Sexual Orientation." *Canadian Pediatric Society* 13, no. 7 (September 2008): 619-23.

"Laser Tattoo Removal." Web MD. Accessed May 1, 2016. http://www.webmd.com/skin-problems-and-treatments/laser-tattoo-removal.

Lyddane, Donald. "Understanding Ganges and Gang Mentality: Acquiring Evidence of the Gang Conspiracy." United States Department of Justice. May 2006. Accessed April 30, 2016. https://www.justice.gov/archive/olp/pdf/gangs.pdf.

"National Youth Gang Survey Analysis." National Gang Center. Accessed July 24, 2016. https://www.nationalgangcenter.gov/survey-analysis/demographics.

Paytasheva, Kristina. "The Emo Subculture—The Dangerous Saving Life Emotion." *Fashion Lifestyle Magazine*. June 2015. Accessed April 30, 2016. http://www.fashion-lifestyle.bg/subculture_en_broi11.

"Piercing? Stick to Earlobe." Web MD. October 24, 2002. Accessed May 1, 2016. http://www.webmd.com/skin-problems-and-treatments/news/20021024/piercing-stick-to-earlobe.

Ryan, Caitlin, David Huebner, Rafael M. Diaz, and Jorge Sanchez. "Family rejection as a predictor of negative health outcomes in white and Latino lesbian, gay, and bisexual young adults." *Pediatrics* 123, no. 1 (2009): 346-352.

Savin-Williams, Ritch C., and Lisa M. Diamond. "Sexual identity trajectories among sexual-minority youths: Gender comparisons." *Archives of Sexual Behavior* 29, no. 6 (2000): 607-627.

Shaw, Rise, ed. *Not Child's Play: An Anthology on Brother-Sister Incest.* Lunchbox Press, 2000.

Sulloway, Frank J. "Birth order, sibling competition, and human behavior." *In Conceptual Challenges in Evolutionary Psychology*, pp. 39-83. Springer Netherlands, 2001.

Sutter, John D. "Survey: 70% of Teens Hide Online Behavior from Parents." CNN. June 25, 2012. Accessed April 30, 2016. http://www.cnn.com/2012/06/25/tech/web/mcafee-teen-online-survey/.

"The Secret Meanings Of Tattoos." National Public Radio. July 30, 2013. Accessed May 1, 2016. http://www.npr.org/sections/theprotojournalist/2013/07/30/203681761/the-secret-meanings-of-tattoos.

"The Truth Behind Social Networks." Tangient LLC. Accessed July 24, 2016. http://thetruthbehindsocialnetworks.wikispaces.com/Survey+Results?showComments=1

Wharton, Morgan. "Self-injury and Choking: Destructive Behaviors in Children and Teenagers." National Center for Health Research. 2013. Accessed May 1, 2016. http://center4research.org/child-teen-health/suicide/self-injury-and-choking/.

"What Is a Gang? Definitions." National Institute of Justice. Accessed April 30, 2016. http://www.nij.gov/topics/crime/gangs/pages/definitions.aspx.

Wiehe, Vernon R. *Sibling Abuse: Hidden Physical, Emotional, and Sexual Trauma.* Sage Publications, 1997.

Wiehe, Vernon R. *What Parents Need to Know About Sibling Abuse: Breaking the Cycle of Violence.* Bonneville Books, 2002.

Acknowledgments

None of my books would have ever been published without the dedicated, kind, patient, supportive dream team of my illustrator, Jack Varonin; graphic designer, Casey Brodhead, PsyD; editor, Mark Burstein; Gail Kearns, my publicist who has been such a help and support; Kathy Moran, my Web designer has been unbelievably creative in designing a unique and user-friendly site; and publisher, Andrew Benzie. Honestly, I am just the scribe, but you six are the creators, the people who have made my writings come alive. I shall always be so humbly grateful for your expertise, confidence in our product, hard work, availability, advice, and feedback. If my "thank yous" were all placed in a bucket and each were worth a dollar, it would be equivalent to paying off the national debt!

About the Author

Dr. Ann Schiebert has vast experience with teens, adults, and families in the area of chemical dependence, codependency, dual diagnosis, and trauma. She has spent years designing ways in which families and couples can have a more harmonious relationship based on making agreements with each other. Dr. Schiebert also teaches couple's communication and codependency recovery classes. The communication "scripts" that her patients learn have been time tested and have assisted them in alleviating interaction styles that create contention.

In addition to her work at the Walnut Creek, California, mental health clinic of a major national HMO, Dr. Schiebert works in its emergency department and hospital as a psychiatric crisis specialist. She also has a private practice that specializes in codependency issues. This is the second volume of her Let's Make a Contract tetralogy: *Getting Your Teen Through Substance Abuse* was published in 2016 and *Getting Through Unhappy Romantic Relationships* was published in 2018.

Dr. Schiebert is the mother of three adult children and lives with her partner, Tom Rohrer, PhD, in Lafayette, California.

A Note From the Author

If you enjoyed this book, I would greatly appreciate a short review on Amazon or your favorite book website. As an author, reviews are critical to our success, so even a line or two can make a difference.

Also, I hope you'll consider signing up for my mailing list to receive occasional updates about the Let's Make a Contract series and future projects in development. Simply go to: https://www.drannschiebert.com

As always, I welcome any other comments or questions you may have and can be reached at: ann@drannschiebert.com

Books Available in the
Let's Make a Contract Series

 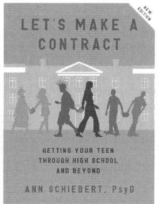  

Let's Make a Contract Books:
Getting Your Teen Through Substance Abuse
Getting Your Teen Through High School and Beyond
Getting Through Unhappy Romantic Relationships
Getting Your Teen Past the Opioid Epidemic

For more information, please visit:
www.drannschiebert.com

Made in the USA
San Bernardino, CA
16 January 2019